PATTI POTTER

FAKE CHRISTIANS

WOLVES IN SHEEP'S CLOTHING WHO ARE
IMPERILING AMERICAN DEMOCRACY

STUDIO
OF BOOKS
THE SPACE FOR YOUR MESSAGE

Copyright © 2024 by Patti Potter

All rights reserved. No part of this publication may be reproduced, distributed, or transmitted in any form or by any means, including photocopying, recording, or other electronic or mechanical methods, without the prior written permission of the copyright owner and the publisher, except in the case of brief quotations embodied in critical reviews and certain other noncommercial uses permitted by copyright law. For permission requests, write to the publisher, "Attention: Permissions Coordinator," to the address below.

Studio of Books LLC
5900 Balcones Drive Suite 100
Austin, Texas 78731
www.studioofbooks.org
Hotline: (254) 800-1183

Ordering Information:
Special discounts are available on quantity purchases by corporations, associations, and others. For details, contact the publisher at the address above.

Printed in the United States of America.

ISBN-13: Softcover   978-1-968491-04-8
          Ebook   978-1-968491-05-5

Library of Congress Control Number: 2025913294

Fake Christians
The Wolves in Sheep's Clothing Who are Imperiling American Democracy

By Patti Potter

"The book is an easy read about complex issues in our society. It is how people in authority can bend the laws and ignore the truth when it is to their advantage and benefit. Unfortunately we have a lot of human-shaped creatures that don't act like humans in our society. We still have a long way to go. Thank you for your book."

-Mandana Zolghadr

"This book is an unfiltered and deeply honest account of the author's personal experiences growing up. It sheds light on topics often spoken of in hushed tones, offering readers a rare glimpse into realities that many may find eye-opening. The author's journey, from childhood to navigating the complexities of the present day, is both powerful and thought-provoking. A truly remarkable read that leaves a lasting impression."

-Anonymous

"Patti does a fantastic job of exposing the facts about people who claim to be Christians, but whose words and actions certainly don't reflect the teachings or actions of Jesus."

-Anonymous

Dedication

To my family and all the good people who are standing up to the evil, hypocritical forces out there.

Author's Note

This book was inspired by the hypocrisy I witness daily from the MAGA Republican evangelical Christians and other so-called religious groups. It is not a rebuke of real Christians and others who actually practice what they preach. Some of the names in the personal history sections of this book have been changed.

Contents

Me as a Toddler

Woe to you, scribes and Pharisees, hypocrites! For you build the tombs of the prophets and decorate the monuments of the righteous.

– Matthew 23:29

And the haters gonna hate, hate, hate, hate, hate Baby, I'm just gonna shake, shake, shake, shake, shake I shake it off, I shake it off

– Taylor Swift

Chapter 1

"Teach Your Children Well"
Crosby, Stills, Nash, and Young

Growing Up Catholic

First day of first grade

"In school today, Bobby was accused by the nun for mumbling. Then she was hitting him, and he said, 'I'm getting out of this f**kn place. you f**kn asshole!'"

This incident was recorded in my eighth-grade diary (1969– 1970).

Note: I was afraid to write the actual word "fuck" because then I would be obligated to go to confession. After entering the dark wooden confessional box, I would start by reciting, "Bless me, Father, for I have sinned." Then I would report my transgression(s) and show my contrition by doing a penance, which might be to recite two Our Fathers, three Hail Marys, and the Act of Contrition, and then pray the Rosary.

We were required to attend confession every two weeks, even if we hadn't "sinned." If we had committed the same sin more than once, we had to give an exact account of our transgressions. Sometimes, I would make up a number because I hadn't counted them. A common confession might be, "I disobeyed my father five times."

Recently, a neighbor shared a story about his wife growing up Catholic: "She was a very rule-abiding, good person. When she was a little kid, she went into confession one day but had nothing to confess and ask forgiveness for. When she told the priest, he said he didn't believe her and that she must have done something bad. She insisted that she hadn't. The priest got more aggressive and told her that, surely, she had cheated in school. My wife got confused. She thought maybe she was supposed to lie, cheat, steal, and then confess afterward. So, she lied to the priest and told him she had cheated. The priest was happy, and her penance was a bunch of Hail Marys.

Bobby, the subject of my eighth-grade diary entry, was a classmate at my suburban Philadelphia elementary school. He was one of the few Black kids at the school. Our teacher, a nun, used various unholy techniques to punish him for minor indiscretions.

Sometimes, the nun pushed Bobby into the cloakroom that housed our school bags and coats. There, he was ordered to think and pray about what he had done and seek God's forgiveness. After the nun closed the folding doors behind him, we could hear his ignored cries to be let out. They lasted for what seemed like an eternity.

I witnessed and experienced physical and emotional abuse by nuns and priests regularly during my twelve years of Catholic schooling. As a result, I have a very low tolerance for those who pretend to be followers of the Lord but do bad things. The recent rise of MAGA followers pretending to be evangelical "Christians," even though their words and actions are anything but Christian, has brought back a lot of memories for me.

This book connects my personal history to our present challenges to help thwart the hypocrites threatening American democracy.

Chapter 2

"Movin' on Up"

Our split-level home in the Philadelphia suburbs

My dad was so proud to be able to buy a split-level home with a large backyard. Split-level homes (a variation of ranch homes) became popular after World War II. Builders were able to fit many of these homes and yards into existing neighborhoods, giving families a sense of community. Our neighborhood consisted of families like ours, with working dads and stay-at-home moms. Our world revolved around the Catholic Church. That was the other thing my dad was proud of: raising his kids to be devout Catholics.

My dad worked as a driver-salesman for an Italian bakery in Philadelphia. He delivered loaves of bread and sweets to restaurants and stores in the city before they opened for business. He worked six nights a week. On a typical day, he would leave our house around midnight and drive downtown to pick up and deliver the daily orders. He would return home around eleven the next morning, bringing a bag of freshly baked Italian rolls. They smelled so good! He would eat the delicious lunch my mom had prepared. Then he'd nap, wake up to watch the evening news and eat dinner, take another nap, and start all over again. My sister and I were reprimanded if we were too noisy.

As a kid, I found my neighborhood magical. We rode bikes, went roller skating and bowling, and frequented the nearby amusement park. In the winter, we went sledding on a hill in the neighborhood. Both my parents attended Mass every Sunday. My dad liked the 7:30 a.m. service because the priest "gets you in and out fast." My mom, my sister, and I would go later. I was so happy when, after the Second Vatican Council, Pope John XXIII allowed Mass to be said in the vernacular, or local language, rather than Latin. This allowed churchgoers to understand the service and thus to better participate in it. In the '70s, our parish church started offering a guitar Mass every Sunday. My friends and I loved hearing the beautiful folk songs and singing along to them. It was much more fun than listening to the church organ and Latin words I didn't understand.

My mom did what most women in our neighborhood at the time did. She stayed home to care for her family. My mom relished the role. In addition to being an amazing cook, she encouraged my sister and me to become our best selves. We took piano lessons and became Girl Scouts. Magical times were spent listening to Mom read books. We'd start our days with breakfast while Mom read to us. When we came home for lunch before heading back to school, Mom was always waiting with a wonderful meal and more reading while we ate.

You would probably label my mom a "rebel." Most of the mothers in our neighborhood, who (like Mom) were raised by Italian immigrants, covered their living room sofas and chairs with plastic. The covering supposedly would help preserve the furniture's material. One neighbor had wall-to-wall carpeting installed in the family garage. My mom thought the covers would make the furniture uncomfortable (true) and wondered why anyone would carpet a garage. She was not a follower.

She also loved throwing amazing birthday parties for my sister and me.

Mom was a lover of all kinds of music, from Frank Sinatra to Janis Joplin. She took my sister and me to live concerts to see the Four Seasons and other rock and roll performers. I loved hearing stories about Mom's bus trips from Philadelphia to New York City as a teenager to see her favorite entertainers perform live. She was thrilled when my friends and I got to see Sinatra at the Spectrum in Philadelphia when I was eighteen years old.

Watching the Beatles debut on The Ed Sullivan Show on the black-and-white TV in our living room was one of the highlights of my life. I'm forever grateful to my mom for exposing me to the best of popular culture.

Chapter 3

"Take a look / It's in a book / A reading rainbow"

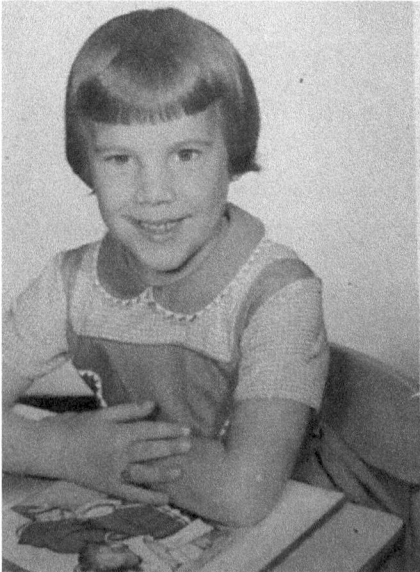

A booklover from kindergarten to the present day

I started reading at age four. Nobody formally taught me. Part of the credit goes to my mom for emphasizing the importance of reading. She was an avid reader and read to us every day and night. My parents were so proud of me. They bragged about me to friends and family and would often have me show off by reading books to them when they visited. My dad encouraged me to read aloud the outdoor signs of stores and restaurants that we passed by on car rides.

The other important thing that happened when I was four years old was that my mom bought me the very first Barbie doll ever made. I began collecting the other dolls and accessories as soon as they came out. I loved lining my Barbie dolls up as if they were in a classroom and reading to them. I'd invite my friends over and pretend to be a teacher. You'd have probably labeled me as "bossy." (I probably still am!) I always knew I would become a teacher.

Later, after I received a bachelor's degree in elementary education and a master's degree in gifted education, I was able to spend a large part of my career teaching kids who were not always understood by their parents and teachers. This had been my own experience. A lot of them were bored in their classrooms, and as a result, they tuned out or had behavior problems.

Looking back, I remember being so excited to begin kindergarten at four and a half. The rule then was that kindergarteners needed to turn five by the end of their enrollment year. My birthday is November 29, which made me the youngest student in my class. The Catholic school in our neighborhood didn't have a kindergarten, so I attended public school for that one year.

One morning before leaving for kindergarten, Mom excitedly urged me to bring "The Cat in the Hat" by Dr. Seuss to school so I could read it to the class. When I asked Mrs. Doyle if I could read my book to the class, she rolled her eyes and said yes. Taking a seat in front of my classmates who sat before me on the rug, I began: "The sun did not shine. It was too wet to play. So we sat in the house. All that cold, cold, wet day." I read with expression and used different voices for the characters. When I finished, all my classmates clapped.

When my classmates returned to their seats, Mrs. Doyle called me to sit beside her desk. "You can't read," she said. "You're only four and a half." She turned the book to the last page and said smugly, "Now read it backward." I was confused but started with the last word in the book and read it in reverse. Because it's a rhyming book, she assumed that I'd just memorized it but didn't really know how to read the words. I got home and cried to my mom about what had happened. She immediately called the school to speak to Mrs. Doyle and set her straight. Thanks, Mom!

I made it through kindergarten despite being bored to death. One of the highlights of my younger years was when the bookmobile came through our neighborhood. A few years later, the town library opened.

Today's book banners are like the hypocrites I encountered as a curious kid. You can imagine my horror when book bans recently began surging in schools and neighborhood libraries around our country. Groups like Moms for Liberty that pretend to have their children's best interest at heart advocate for these bans. According to a report by the free speech group PEN America, such efforts are aimed at "the suppression of stories and ideas." During the 2022–2023 school year, PEN America found 3,362 cases of book bans, up from 2,532 bans in the 2021–2022 school year. Florida had more bans than any other state.

In February 2024, during Black History Month, a K–8 school in Miami named Coral Way required parents to sign a permission slip to allow their kids to "participate and listen to a book written by an African American." The form didn't reveal the title or author of the book. The sole cause for possible concern appeared to be the author's blackness. This requirement complies with the state's 2022 Individual Freedom Act (a.k.a. the Stop WOKE Act), which controls how race can be taught in schools. Another Florida bill passed that year, the Parental Rights in Education Law (a.k.a. the "Don't Say Gay" Law), does the same thing for sexual orientation and gender identity.

The adjective "woke" was officially added to the Oxford English Dictionary in June 2017. It initially meant "well-informed, up to date," but now usually means "alert to racial or social discrimination and injustice." The Urban Dictionary published its definition two years earlier: "Being woke means being aware . . . knowing what's going on in the community (related to racism and social injustice)." In other words, it means to be awake to sensitive social issues, such as racism.

A USA Today/Ipsos poll published in March 2023 shows that Americans interpret the meaning of "woke" in different ways. When asked what it means to be "woke," a majority defined it as being informed about social injustices rather than being politically correct. Democrats and younger Americans were more likely to see "wokeness" as a compliment, while Republicans and older Americans understood it as an insult.

Recently, Republican candidate for Missouri Secretary of State Valentina Gomez posted a video of herself using a flamethrower to incinerate two public library books. "When I'm Secretary of State," Gomez posted on X, "I will BURN all books that are grooming, indoctrinating, and sexualizing our children. MAGA. America First." The two books Gomez burned are Sex Ed books: "Naked: Not Your Average Sex Book," by Myriam Daguzan Bernier, and "Queer: The Ultimate LGBTQ Guide for Teens," by Kathy Belge and Marke Bieschke.

Khaled Hosseini, author of the much-banned 2003 novel "The Kite Runner," said in an interview:

"In a democracy, children should learn that they're going to share the world with people who may look and speak differently than they do, and they may hold different value systems than they do. And those people are deserving of the same rights, respect, and dignity as everyone else. Books are a conduit for that sort of learning. When they're banned, it's damaging because restricting access to them keeps schools from doing one of their defining jobs, which is to prepare students for the duties and responsibilities and the challenges of being citizens."

Banning books is like banning democracy itself.

Chapter 4

"Another Brick in the Wall"

Me as a Junior Girl Scout at age nine

The rest of my school days were spent being taught by both nuns and lay Catholic school teachers. Some teachers were straight out of Catholic high schools and attended college classes in the evening. The nuns at that time didn't have college degrees, but many of the lay teachers earned their college degrees by taking classes in the evenings. In first grade, there were about sixty students in my class. We were taught by a nun. Our desks were arranged in straight rows based on how well we did on the school's placement test. I was placed in the first row, but I can't imagine how the kids in the last row felt about why they were put there.

Because I was already a proficient reader, the books about Dick and Jane were so dull. I would finish a book, tell Sister, and then be told to sit down and read it again. If I finished a worksheet or a test before my classmates, I was made to sit down, erase my answers, and redo the worksheet, which I obediently did. Meanwhile, I was going crazy!!

I was frequently reprimanded for talking and passing notes to my friends. The nuns would call my parents, and I would get a lecture. At that time, most neighborhood parents had high respect for the nuns and priests and tended to take a nun's word over their kid's. My dad used to deliver cakes free of charge from his bakery to the convent and rectory for the nuns and priests.

My report cards from my elementary school years show mostly A's in academic areas. My dad loved to carry around my First and Second Honors cards to show his friends and family members. When my Self-Control grade dropped to a "C" one year, my father freaked out. I told him, "But Dad, I got all A's except for that!"

Later in life, I realized how much my boredom contributed to my behavior issues. I finished my work quickly and had nothing to do, so I would talk to and pass notes to my classmates.

Outside of school, I was definitely not bored. My extra-curricular activities in grade school included Girl Scouts, piano lessons, dancing to the television show "American Bandstand" (hosted by Dick Clark and filmed in Philadelphia), and hanging out with friends in the neighborhood.

One year, the school had a Tag Day. This was a day when we contributed to a local charity and were rewarded by getting to wear non-uniform clothes. On a shopping trip with my mom, I had chosen what I thought was a great outfit. I woke up on Tag Day morning so excited. I put on my miniskirt and white go-go boots and walked to school. As soon as I walked into the classroom, Sister told me I was dressed inappropriately. She told me to go back home, change into my uniform, and then come back to school, which I grudgingly did.

In eighth grade, I entered and won first prize in the Archdiocese of Philadelphia's religious vocation booklet contest. Each student who entered chose a specific order of nuns or priests to research and then created a booklet showing its history, work, and daily routines. The hope was that we would consider a vocation to the sisterhood or priesthood in the future. For some strange reason, I chose to create my booklet about a cloistered order. Cloistered nuns are devoted to the service of God and people. They live in a place cut off from the rest of the world and only leave the cloister for medical emergencies. These nuns take vows of chastity, poverty, enclosure, and obedience, and follow the rule of silence most of the day. The rest of the time is mostly spent in worship and prayer. Today, this is referred to as the "contemplative life," in contrast to the "active life" of the noncloistered orders. I was fascinated by this lifestyle but had already decided I wouldn't be a nun. For starters, I liked to talk too much to be able to maintain silence for long periods of time.

As the first-place winner, I was honored at a school Mass. I couldn't wait to see what my prize would be. My friend Annie, sitting next to me, whispered, "I bet it's a Barbie doll." I was so hoping it was because I loved Barbie dolls. When my name was called, I left the pew and nervously approached the altar. After a short speech by the priest, I was presented with my first-place prize, a Sacred Heart of Jesus statue. The school was gifted with a set of vestments (liturgical garments) by the organization that sponsored the contest. Later, I joined the other four top winners at a luncheon in our honor in the city.

Another reason the contemplative life was not for me was that I was always interested in what was happening in the world around me. Several national tragedies occurred while I was in elementary school. I'll never forget finding out about the senseless deaths of John F. Kennedy on November 22, 1963, Robert F. Kennedy on June 6, 1968, and Martin Luther King, Jr. on April 4, 1969.

I remember asking my mom at one point, "Are they going to keep killing people?" She assured me that these were rare instances.

Vocation booklet winners' luncheon
(I'm second from the left, seated.)

I was also exposed to the pervasive racism toward Blacks in Philadelphia and its suburbs. If a white family was selling their house, they made sure they didn't sell to a Black family. "There goes the neighborhood" was a familiar refrain if someone did sell their house to a family that wasn't white.

One Saturday in fifth grade, I was at a nearby bowling alley with my friends. Some Black kids who were there invited us to shoot pool with them. When my dad came to pick us up and saw who we were with, he yelled, "Why are you hanging out with these ni**ers?!" I got a long lecture when we got home about how bad Black people are and how I should never hang out with any of them again. I felt so sad for the kids who had heard his angry tirade and racial slurs. Despite my dad's sentiments, my friends were quite a diverse group of people (happily, the same is true today).

In August 1964, when I was in elementary school, the Columbia Avenue Riots occurred in North Philadelphia. There had been tensions between Black residents and police officers in the city because of documented cases of police brutality toward Blacks. This was one of the first of the so-called "ghetto riots" of the '60s.

The rioting lasted from Friday to Sunday. Protesters vandalized and looted businesses owned by whites. Two people were killed, 350 were wounded, and the total damage to businesses on Columbia Avenue was approximately $4 million (or $40 million in today's dollars). Over one thousand people were arrested, and many others were beaten by police officers. In 1964, Blacks made up 18 percent of Philadelphia's population but were 40 percent of the inmates in area jails and prisons.

Columbia Avenue Riots arest

Frank Rizzo joined the Philadelphia Police Department in 1943. In the '50s, he was known for raiding gay and beatnik clubs. At the end of the subsequent decade, Rizzo became Philadelphia's police commissioner. Soon after, he was elected as mayor, a position he held between 1972 and 1980. During his time as mayor, the U.S. Department of Justice filed a lawsuit against the city's police department, saying officers' use of excessive force "shocks the conscience." A lot of white people liked Rizzo's "tough guy" persona, while others called him a racist. My dad was a fan of Rizzo. As someone who worked nights in the city, my dad felt the mayor was making the city safer.

Philadelphia's Frank L. Rizzo Monument, a bronze sculpture of the former mayor, was installed in 1998. It was removed in June, 2020 when, during the George Floyd protests, Black Lives Matter activists and others protested the statue's presence.

There are a lot of similarities between Frank Rizzo and Donald Trump. In a November, 2020 article in the Philadelphia Inquirer, Will Bunch wrote, "Many before me have noticed the uncanny Trump- Rizzo similarities, especially the strong-man 'law-and-order' posture and their shared hatred of political correctness." Rizzo famously pledged to "make Atilla the Hun look like a faggot." His use of highly offensive language shows what made him a flashpoint. It was this tradition of verbal outrage that Trump later adapted to his often xenophobic twenty-first-century agenda. This is another unfortunate connection between my personal history and our present times.

Chapter 5

"Rock and Roll High School"

Me in my high school uniform at age thirteen

My after-school vibe

During my eight long, boring years in Catholic grade school, I personally witnessed nuns and priests physically and emotionally abuse children. Friends from those days have told me about their own experiences, including nuns taking prohibited gum out of a student's mouth and tangling it in her hair and nuns who violently removed pierced earrings out of girls' ears. I was ready to move on.

I was excited to start high school and hoped things would be better there. I was disappointed on that front, perhaps because it, too, was a Catholic school. In my freshman year, our school was segregated by gender. Boys were on one side of the building, girls on the other. There were separate entry doors for each group. Sometimes, through the walls, we could hear priests physically beating and berating the boys. One of my high school classmates shared a memory about observing a nun banging a girl's head against a locker and pulling out some of her hair in the process.

Based on my academic abilities, I was placed in Track 1 and Honors classes. In my sophomore year, our school decided to integrate our school, with boys and girls in the same classes. The integration that first year was only for Honors and Track 1 students. Apparently, they assumed (wrongly) that "smart" kids wouldn't be attracted to the opposite sex. If things worked out with us, we were told, they would implement the plan for all students the following year (which they did).

There was a lot going on in our country during my high school years. The counterculture movement of the '60s started when young people rejected the conventional social norms of the '50s regarding race relations, the Cold War, and women's rights.

As with grade school, our high school classes were taught by nuns from various religious orders along with lay teachers. Lay teachers are not part of the ordained clergy and are not ordained education. Thanks to this, I had several amazing lay teachers in high school.

Our English teacher, Mr. Jones, encouraged us to bring record albums to play in class and then engage in interesting discussions about the meaning of the lyrics. Sometimes students would sneak an album into class that contained explicit lyrics and/or sexual content, then pretend they didn't know in advance. I remember one day a classmate named Tommy brought the Woodstock album and asked Mr. Jones to play the protest song, "I-Feel-Like-I'm-Fixin'-to-Die Rag" by Country Joe and the Fish. We all knew how the song started: "Give me an F! Give me a U! Give me a C! Give me a K! What's that spell?" We all started chanting "the word." Mr. Jones looked surprised and quickly took it off the classroom turntable. I worried that Tommy would be sent to the principal, but he told the boy to put it in his school bag and never bring it back. I should have reported "saying a bad word" to the priest at my next confession, but I didn't. Mr. Jones was a big fan of Simon and Garfunkel. He loved playing songs from the album "Sounds of Silence." We did too!

During my high school years, I continued to lead an active life. I participated in the chorus and French Club. In eleventh grade, I auditioned for and got a part in our school's performance of "The Music Man." I also had various part-time jobs during these years. One was at a donut shop in town. The owner-manager was a creepy old man who liked to fondle the teenage girls who worked there. When I told my mom about it, she made me quit immediately.

I worked at a W. T. Grant department store as a part-time clerk/cashier. I was soon promoted to a part-time position in the main office of the store. One of the managers, Johnny, was shady. He was married and in his thirties. Sometimes when I was working the register, he would put on the conveyor belt a shitload of store merchandise that was already in store bags. Without opening the bags, he would tell me how much to ring up. It was clear he was stealing from the store. He would also ask the stock boys to take furniture out through the back stock room door and have them help him load it in his truck. He also started a clandestine relationship with one of the teenage girls I worked with. His wife found out, and Johnny ended the relationship with the girl (I think).

My favorite job was as a "candy girl" at the refreshment counter of a movie theater. The perks were great! We were permitted to watch movies for free when we weren't working. But sometimes we'd also help ourselves to popcorn from the large bin at the counter. We made sure we didn't get caught. I also worked as a babysitter and tutor. It was getting clearer to me that I loved kids and would be a teacher one day.

The best extracurricular activities were the ones I participated in outside of school hours. Our parents, who had grown up in the city, raised us like city kids. We had free rein to do what we wanted during the day as long as we came home at night.

Along with regularly attending the school's football and basketball games and dances, my friends and I enjoyed bowling, roller skating, and going to see the latest movies. Some of my favorites were "Easy Rider," "2001: A Space Odyssey," "Butch Cassidy and the Sundance Kid," "Airplane," and "Romeo and Juliet." I was so in love with Leonard Whiting (Romeo) that I had a poster of him in my room and wrote him many fan letters (sadly, I received no response).

Neighborhood kids would take turns hosting parties at their homes on weekend nights, where unbeknownst to our parents, we'd play spin the bottle, smoke weed, and listen to the latest record albums. Whenever I went out, I had to make sure I got home before my dad woke up for work around midnight. One night, I was late and was sitting in my boyfriend's car after a date. We were making out. Suddenly, we heard someone banging on the car window. It was my dad, and he wasn't happy. He yelled at us and told me to "get the hell in the house!"

We would drive to the Spectrum or the Tower Theater in Philadelphia to see our favorite performers live. It was so exciting to see Elvis Presley (during his last tour), Queen, David Bowie, the Rolling Stones, Yes, Pink Floyd, Chicago, the Eagles, and many others. I loved (and still love) rock music so much and would play the newest albums on the turntable in my bedroom. I'd close the door, but the music could be heard throughout the house. Once, my dad got so mad that he took the door off the hinges, and I had no door to my bedroom for a few months.

In the '70s, I became a huge David Bowie fan. He was the antithesis of what was being preached in our church and high school. His Ziggy Stardust persona helped to define the Glam Rock movement of the time. Ziggy was an androgynous alien character whose songs and stage presence were captivating. In July, 1974, when I found out that Bowie would be performing at the Tower Theater as part of his *Diamond Dogs* tour, I knew I had to go.

Before Ticketmaster and other online ticket sale companies existed, we would bring sleeping bags and line up outside a local record store in Philly the night before tickets went on sale. We wanted to make sure we got tickets before the show sold out. It was great hanging out with others who also loved the artist or band you wanted to see live. The booze and illicit marijuana some fans brought and shared made the experience almost as good as the concert itself.

Early in the morning of the Bowie ticket sale, while it was still dark, I saw a familiar-looking bakery delivery truck slowly go by and stop on the street where we were lined up. I got the tickets, but I also got a long lecture later that day about going to a David Bowie show. Didn't I know he was a "faggot?" My response ("It doesn't matter, Dad. He's good.") didn't go over well.

The Bowie concert was a truly unforgettable experience, and I swear I can hear myself screaming loudly in joy on the concert album "David Live."

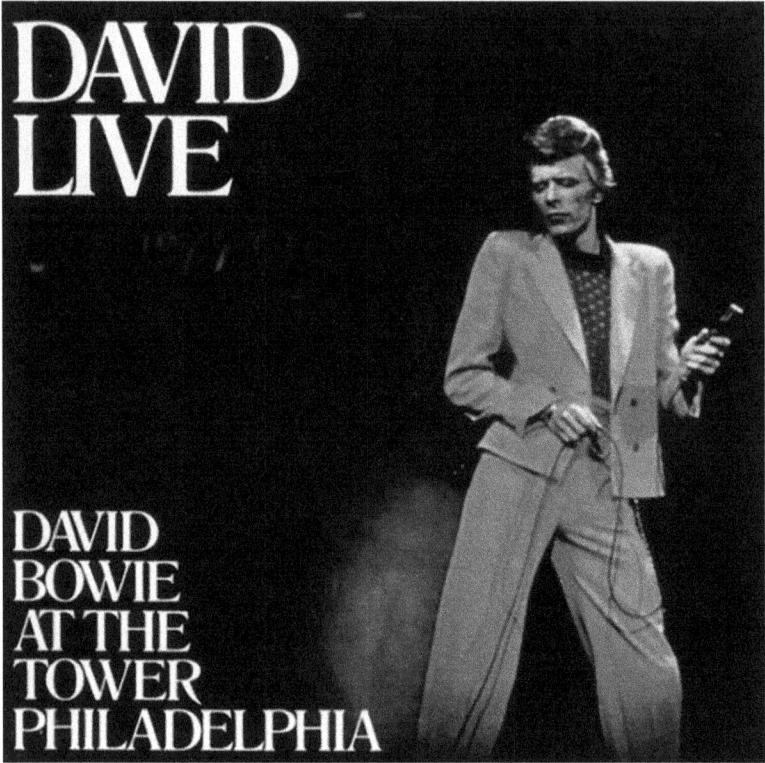

One of the highlights of my life was taking my then twenty-two-year-old son to a David Bowie concert in 2004 during his Reality Tour.

After Bowie died in 2016, I visited a tattoo shop and got this amazing artwork. My dad used to say, "Only sailors and whores get tattoos," He would have hated it!

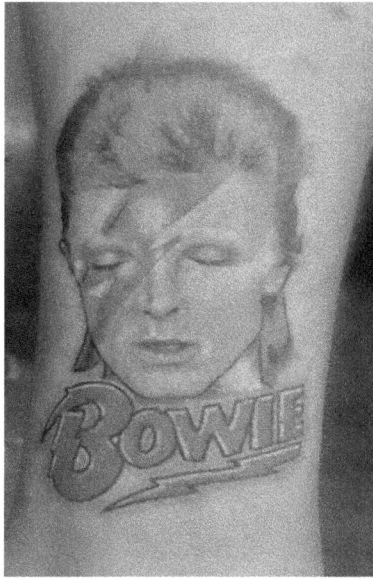

Most of the boys I dated in high school attended public schools. My first "real" boyfriend, Sammy, was a dropout from one of those schools. He worked full-time at a restaurant. I soon realized that the things the nuns told us NOT to do were a lot of fun. As Billy Joel sang, "Only the good die young."

When Sammy first broached the subject of sex, I firmly said, "I'm not that kind of girl." Then I learned from other girls at school that there was a local doctor who would prescribe birth control pills (no questions asked). Being the responsible girl I was, I got a prescription. On January 22, 1973 (my senior year), the Roe v. Wade decision came down. My friends were relieved that they had a choice if they got pregnant. I had several other boyfriends in high school, including a biker who'd give me rides on his Harley-Davidson motorcycle.

Back then, I devised ways to do things that the hypocritical adults in my life told me not to. Specifically, my friends and I looked for any opportunity to read the books and see the movies that the Legion of Decency condemned. The National Legion of Decency was established in 1933 and then reorganized in 1965 as the National Catholic Office for Motion Pictures (NCOMP). The group rated films based on their suitability for viewing. Films were given a code of A, B, or C. Being rated C meant the movie was "condemned" for viewing by Catholics.

Over the years, my friends and I saw such "condemned" movies as "Valley of the Dolls," "Rosemary's Baby," "I Am Curious (Yellow)," "The Happy Hooker," and "Everything You Always Wanted to Know about Sex* (*But Were Afraid to Ask). Meanwhile, the boys managed to read Playboy magazine (no doubt for the articles) by getting someone older to buy them a copy at a local store, or by checking their dads' closets. There was a public-school boy whose mom was divorced. I'm not sure why, but she allowed Tommy to invite friends over to their apartment to watch "stag reels" on their home movie projector. Previously, the only home movies I had seen were my dad's films of our summer vacations and Christmas celebrations. Watching porn at Tommy's house seemed a lot safer than going to an "adult" theater at the time.

In 1978, the rating system changed to remove the "condemned" label. The movies that previously would have been rated B or C are now all rated O ("morally offensive"). NCOMP changed its ratings of old films to align with the new system. Thus, it is impossible to determine from the NCOMP database whether a film that is now classified as O was originally B or C.

Needless to say, the ratings made us more eager to see the "condemned" films. We emerged from such experiences untraumatized. They were part of the coming-of-age process.

We had many adventures back then. Since we lived within driving distance of the Jersey Shore, our families would take us to one of the beach towns near Atlantic City for a week's vacation. During our last year of high school, 1973, we excitedly planned our Senior Week vacation (no parents) to Ocean City, New Jersey. Although the legal drinking age in New Jersey had changed in 1973 from 21 to 18, and we all had fake IDs, Ocean City was, and still is, a "dry" town. We knew that we could go to the nearby "wet" town if we needed to get booze, but we were worried about getting arrested. Our parents would have been so mad!

One of my clever friends, Connie, told us that her older brother, who was 21, would be happy to buy us whatever we wanted at the liquor store nearby to take on our trip. She even created a paper order form for us to fill out. We'd pay Joshua after we got the stuff. One day, we began passing around and filling out the form in one of our classes. By senior year, we had become experts in the fine art of passing notes without getting caught. Not this time.

The nun intercepted the form and read what it said. Since the form had been passed to me, she took me out in the hall and lectured me. "You're such a good student and good Catholic girl," she said "You'll never amount to anything unless you straighten yourself out." We still managed to get the booze.

High school graduation

My academic grades were great, but my Self-Control grades were not. I graduated with honors in 1973 and went on to attend Penn State University. During my college years, I was, as always, attracted to "fun" people. My mom suggested that I join a sorority. I went to one meeting and knew it wasn't for me. The activities seemed so boring and too normal for my tastes

The students I chose to hang out with included part-time rock musicians who performed at a bar in town. I remember hanging out with them at their shared off-campus apartment and listening to the latest music. Once, when it was close to Easter Sunday, one of the boys came out of his bedroom wearing a makeshift crown of thorns and carrying a large wooden cross. He began playing his guitar, and the other guys joined in. The nuns would have hated it. There was also a day each spring called "Gentle Thursday." Students would cut classes, sit in a large open grassy area, smoke weed, and listen to a variety of bands.

I was a very responsible student, who rarely missed a class. One semester I had an 8 a.m. Art History class. At the time I was dating a fraternity boy named Craig. Unlike me, he rarely showed up for class, and when he did, he was always late. During our final exam, Craig ran into the lecture hall, got his exam from our professor, and took a seat next to me. He leaned over and whispered, "Move your test closer so I can copy your answers." I quickly whispered back, "Hell, no! I came to class every day, and I studied." I moved to another seat far away from Craig. We broke up soon after.

I graduated with honors from Penn State and happily soon began my teaching career. I was the first person on either side of my family to attend college, so it was a big deal. As I said good-bye to my parents after they helped me move into my dorm room, my dad shared one of his favorite lines, "Patti, don't forget there are two kinds of smart. You're going to get very "book smart" at college, but never forget your "street smarts."

"I won't, dad," I assured him. And I didn't.

Chapter 6

Christian Hypocrites

Sitting next to my English teacher during senior year

As an adult, when I began to look back on my negative experiences at the hands of people who supposedly worshipped Jesus, I partly attributed those experiences to the times. Maybe people didn't know better, or maybe priests and nuns were given way too much respect and adulation in those days. Regardless, what was obvious to me was that the nuns and priests were not following the words of Jesus that they preached.

But when I started to see stories about the sexual abuse of children by priests all over the country, I saw something that was too damning to try to explain away. I was horrified that the Roman Catholic bishops and cardinals who knew about these offenses allowed the offenders to continue serving as priests and assaulting children. Once their crimes were exposed, the perpetrators were transferred from one parish church to another. Since there were no real repercussions, these priests would continue assaulting children at the parish churches where they were transferred.

Their victims were mostly boys but also girls, some as young as three years old, with the majority between the ages of eleven and fourteen. Starting in the '90s, these cases began receiving media attention in the U.S., Canada, Australia, South America, and most of Europe. The abuse of children by Catholic priests was first brought to public attention in 1985, when a Louisiana priest pleaded guilty to eleven counts of molesting boys.

Pope John Paul II was criticized by representatives of the vic-tims for not responding quickly enough to this crisis in the Catholic Church. Irish singer-songwriter Sinead O'Connor protested against that lack of response when she tore up a picture of the pope on a 1992 episode of Saturday Night Live. Her public protest was praised by critics of the Church and attacked by many Catholics. Her career and life were put in danger. In an interview after the show, O'Connor said she held the Catholic Church responsible for the physical, sexual, and emotional abuse she had suffered as a child.

In 2002, the Boston Globe published a series of eight hundred articles showing the results of an investigation into child sex abuse in the Archdiocese of Boston. This investigation led to five Roman Catholic priests being criminally prosecuted. By 2004 the cardinal who had covered up the abuse had resigned, 150 priests had been accused of sexual abuse, and more than five hundred victims had filed claims of abuse. The

2015 American documentary drama "Spotlight", directed by Tom McCarthy, chronicles the Boston Globe team, the oldest ongoing investigative unit in the U.S. newspaper industry. Journalist Walter Johnson, who edited the Globe series, said the newspaper's reporting "put the match to some very, very dry tinder."

Around 10,000 pages of relevant documents, including many that had gone "missing," were protected by a court confidentiality order. The Globe contested this order. Even though the archdio-cese claimed that it was constitutionally entitled to keep its records confidential, the Globe, with support from the victims' lawyers, argued that the interests of the public overpowered the Church's desire for privacy. While waiting for the decision from the judge, the Globe reporters found evidence of previous abuse and learned that the physical documents had been sealed at the request of the Church.

In late January 2002, the 10,000 pages were finally released. Again, the evidence against the Church was overwhelming: the doctors who assessed the offending priests' mental health were unqualified, and the board that approved their reassignments may have been pressured to do so. Then, on the last day of January, the paper unleashed perhaps the most shocking revelation of all. Over the previous decade, the archdiocese had privately settled sexual abuse claims made by Catholic families against seventy of its priests.

Michael Paulson, who now works as theater reporter for the New York Times, was part of the Globe team and won the Pulitzer Prize in 2003 for his coverage of the abuse scandal. Paulson believes there were three main reasons why the newspaper's reporting left many people horrified and angry:

"First, we got to the documents. We ended up with material relating to more than one hundred priests. We had letters from parents, letters to and from priests, masses of internal church documents showing abusive priests being repeatedly moved. Also, the internet enabled our reporting to be read all over. And I think there was a kind of evolution of culture, a moment in history when people were willing to talk critically about religion. Often in the past that just hasn't been possible."

In June 2002, the United States Conference of Catholic Bishops (USCCB) unanimously approved a Charter for the Protection of Children and Young People. The intention was to show that the Catholic Church in the U.S. was committed to providing a "safe environment" for all children in Church-sponsored activities. U.S. Church officials created specific procedures for handling sexual abuse allegations against lay teachers in Catholic schools, parish staff members, coaches, and other people who represent the Church to young people. The result was a "zero tolerance" policy for sexual abuse. This required every diocese to alert the authorities about allegations, investigate those allegations, and remove the offenders from their duties.

Two years later, A Report on the Crisis in the Catholic Church was released publicly by the National Review Board for the Protection of Children and Young People, established by the USCCB. According to the report, 4,392 U.S. clerics were accused of sexual abuse from 1950–2002. It was later found that 30 percent of these accusations were classified as "unsubstantiated." In other cases, there was no investigation because the accused priest had died. The reported numbers are the only "official" such count by the Catholic Church in its history.

As soon as the report was published, the USSCB quickly denounced the legitimacy of the very National Review Board it had established. Originally, audits and more extensive details were going to follow the report. So far, that has yet to happen.

The Archdiocese of Philadelphia had its own reckoning. The rampant cases of sexual abuse within it were first substantially revealed through a grand jury investigation in 2005. In early 2011, a different grand jury presented extensive new charges against priests active in the archdiocese. In 2012, the guilty plea by priest Edward Avery, trial and conviction of Monsignor William Lynn, and mistrial on charges against James J. Brennan (who later struck a deal to serve probation) followed from the grand jury's inves-tigations. During the following year, Charles Engelhardt and teacher Bernard Shero were tried, convicted, and sentenced to prison. Monsignor Lynn was the first Church official to be convicted in the United States of covering up abuses by other priests in his charge. Other senior Church officials have been criticized extensively for their management of the issue in the archdiocese.

In 2018, a grand jury found that hundreds of Roman Catholic priests in Pennsylvania had molested more than one thousand children—and possibly many more—since the '40s. The grand jury also discovered that this abuse had been covered up. Its report numbered the abusive clergy members at more than three hundred. In almost every case, the statute of limitations had run out. This meant that criminal charges could not be filed. More than one hundred of these priests are now deceased. Many others are retired, have either been put on leave, have been or dismissed from the priesthood.

Following this report, seven of Pennsylvania's eight Catholic dioceses began to implement victim compensation funds. The funds were open to claims for a limited time. According to a 2022 report, the Archdiocese of Philadelphia paid out $78.5 million to 438 claimants. At the end of the 2020–2021 school year, my high school was closed. The closure was blamed on low enrollment figures, but people think the large monetary payments by the Archdiocese of Philadelphia to victims of priest sexual abuse had something to do with it. In August 2023, the Archdiocese of Philadelphia agreed to pay $3.5 million to resolve a former Catholic school student's claim that he was sexually abused by a now-deceased priest two decades before. Shockingly, Church officials knew of previous reports about the offending priest going back to the '70s

Sexual abuse is not a problem only associated with the Catholic Church. Other Christian denominations and religious groups have also been the subject of sexual abuse accusations. These include the Southern Baptist Convention and the Anglican Church. The Mormon Church has had accusations of abuse and was found to have covered up sexual assault within the Boy Scouts of America. The Brooklyn-based Haredi Jewish community was the subject of criticism for failing to report abuse cases.

What do all these cases have in common? Each organization claims that it didn't know the abuses were happening. Generally, each group has a set of rules or policies condemning sexual abuse, but rarely is there ever internal discipline for offenders.

The organization known as SNAP (Survivors Network of Those Abused by Priests) was started in 1988 by Barbara Blaine, who was a victim of priest abuse as an eighth grader at an Ohio Catholic school. When Blaine asked for help from a Toledo bishop, she got nothing. The first SNAP meeting was held in Chicago in 1991, giving abuse survivors a safe place to help themselves and others heal. SNAP has continued to provide support to victims and now has more than 25,000 survivors and supporters in the network. The SNAP website, https://www.snapnetwork.org/, has helpful resources for both sur-vivors and advocates. On the site, victims can safely report abuse to their state's attorney general.

These efforts are helping to repair the damage done by so-called Christians. Unfortunately, there is much work to be done, including in the political system.

Chapter 7

God Made Trump?

Hillary Clinton took this selfie of us at a 2016 rally in Virginia

Meanwhile, the evangelical MAGA crowd continues to give Roman Catholic clergy a run for their money in the category of Most Hypocritical Christians. In January 2024, the night before the Iowa Caucus, Donald Trump shared a bizarre video, titled "God Made Trump," which proclaimed him God's chosen representative on Earth. It sounded funny, but coming from a presidential candidate it made me horrified. How dare he pretend he represents God! "Satan Made Trump" was a more suitable title.

I was a big supporter of Hillary Clinton in the 2016 election. I admired her fortitude, intelligence, experience, and caring nature. She was a huge backer of women's, LGBTQ, and civil rights. Our country, unlike many of our peer nations, has never had a female head of state. It was the honor of a lifetime to volunteer at the National Democratic Convention in Philadelphia and watch as Hillary was introduced by her daughter Chelsea before delivering the nomination acceptance speech.

I attended many rallies for Hillary in the Washington, DC, area, where I now live. At one, I had the opportunity to speak with her briefly. We talked about how great being a grandmother is, as my first grandchild was born the year before. I tried to take a selfie of the two of us, but was so nervous and excited that I did a shitty job. Hillary said, "Here, let me do it." She took the selfie, which, of course, I framed and put in a prominent place in my house.

You can thus imagine my shock when I learned that Trump had beaten Hillary in the presidential election. How could anyone vote for someone so evil and immoral who bragged about his horrible words and actions? The MAGA followers explained their devotion to him by stating that he said the things they wanted to say but had felt the need to keep private for many years.

During his 2016 presidential campaign announcement at Trump Tower, Trump called for a wall to be built at the U.S.-Mexico border to keep out what he referred to as "rapists, criminals, and members of drug cartels."

At the 2016 Democratic National Convention in Philadelphia

As the granddaughter of Italian immigrants, I loved hearing the stories of how they "came over" on the boat from Italy because they had heard that the streets were "paved with gold," and of their ecstatic feelings when they first saw the Statue of Liberty. They worked their asses off in factories when they settled in Philadelphia, where they were subjected to anti-Italian slurs like "wop" and "dago." Despite the odds against them, they succeeded and were very proud to be Americans.

It made me so angry to hear Trump talk about immigrants the way he did. I taught students from many countries and cultures, and I loved hearing their backstories, as well as about their accomplishments since they arrived. How dare Trump generalize that from Mexico are "bad" people and need to be kept out of our country?

There seemed to be bottomless amounts of evil in this person. In August 2015, during the first GOP presidential debate, conservative Fox News anchor Megyn Kelly asked Trump whether referring to women as "fat pigs," "dogs," and "slobs" showed that he may not have the temperament needed to be president. The next day, in a CNN interview, he struck back at Kelly: "You could see there was blood coming out of her eyes, blood coming out of her, wherever." People interpreted the "wherever" as referring to female menstruation. Although the MAGA cultists might have been surprised that Trump was attacking someone from Fox News, they continued to support him.

For a while, many Christian evangelicals and traditional Republicans withheld support for Trump. There were plenty of problems with his campaign, but the MAGA supporters still worshipped him. At an Iowa rally in January 2016, Trump bragged, "I could stand in the middle of 5th Avenue and shoot somebody, and I wouldn't lose voters." What's even scarier is that he probably spoke the truth.

At the Republican National Convention that year, Republicans were united in their hatred of and vitriol against Hillary Clinton. This is where "Lock Her Up!" became a battle cry and slogan. During Trump's first presidential debate with Hillary, he said that he "was going to say something extremely rough to Hillary" but would refrain because her daughter Chelsea was present.

And that wasn't all. In October 2016, a recording surfaced from Trump's "Access Hollywood" TV show appearance in

2005. In the recording, Trump uttered his now-infamous words: "I just start kissing them. It's like a magnet. Just kiss. I don't even wait. And when you're a star, they let you do it. You can do anything…Grab 'em by the pussy. You can do anything."

The weekend after the tape surfaced, Trump's campaign put out a statement calling Trump's misogynistic words "just locker room talk." Trump issued a video "apology." Several prominent Republicans wanted him to end his candidacy following the remarks. Trump used their disapproval as a call to "war." He tweeted, "It is so nice that the shackles have been taken off me and I can now fight for America the way I want to."

At the second debate with Hillary, Trump brought in several women who had accused Bill Clinton of sexual assault and rape. Unfortunately for Trump, the women were not allowed to confront the former president, who was sitting in the audience during the debate.

The remainder of Trump's campaign was spent defaming Hillary and dealing with allegations of sexual assault made by many women. As usual, Trump denied all of them and threatened lawsuits against the women. The newest rally chants were "Drain the Swamp" and "Build the Wall." Although there were some Republicans who didn't support him, Trump played on the GOP's hatred of Hillary and promised to appoint conservative Supreme Court justices who would overturn the Roe v Wade decision that protected women's access to abortion.

We all know what happened on Election Day in 2016. But even scarier are the things that happened later and are still happening now.

Chapter 8

Evangelicals

Black Lives Matter Mural Washington, DC

In "Disloyal", Michael Cohen's 2020 tell-all memoir, the former Trump attorney and fixer quotes Trump as calling Christianity and its practices "bullshit" shortly before pretending to hold to the faith. According to Cohen, "Trump's religion is unbridled lust for money and power at any cost to others." So why the hell are so-called evangelical Christians worshipping at the altar of Trump after his many criminal indictments and un-Christian words and actions?

In "The Kingdom, the Power, and the Glory; American Evangelicals in an Age of Extremism," Tim Alberta, staff writer for the Atlantic and former chief political correspondent for Politico, traces the history of the current evangelical movement to the confluence of religion and politics and explains how the election of Donald Trump and the COVID-19 pandemic helped fan the flames of the anti-woke, anti-vax, gun-toting, misogynistic, racist, homophobic, and book-banning movement. Alberta writes:

"The greater Trump's criminal difficulties—he faced charges for falsifying business records related to the hush money paid to his porn-star paramour, illegally taking national-security secrets to his Florida home (and obstructing justice in the ensuing investigation), and attempting to overthrow the 2020 election, all while fighting a civil case for rape and defamation—the greater his support from evangelical Christians."

WTF???!

Racial politics only intensified the evangelical love affair with Trump. On May 25, 2020, George Floyd, a forty-six-year-old Black man, was murdered by forty-four-year-old white police officer Derek Chauvin in Minneapolis. The incident was brought to the public's attention when bystander videos were released. Floyd had been arrested for allegedly using a counterfeit $20 bill at a store. While Floyd was lying face down on the street in handcuffs, Chauvin knelt on his neck for over nine minutes. Two officers helped to restrain

Floyd, one officer pointed a gun at Floyd's head before he was handcuffed, and another kept bystanders from trying to intervene. On December 15, 2021, Chauvin pleaded guilty to willfully depriving George Floyd of his constitutional rights while acting under color of law, resulting in Mr. Floyd's bodily injury and death.

The horrific murder of George Floyd became a rallying cry for the Black Lives Matter (BLM) movement, which began in 2013 with the hashtag #BlackLivesMatter appearing on social media outlets. It was the result of the acquittal of George Zimmerman in the shooting death of African American teenager Trayvon Martin. The movement gained recognition the following year for street demonstrations after the deaths of two African Americans: Michael Brown in Ferguson, Missouri, and Eric Garner in New York City.

On June 1, 2020, during the George Floyd protests in Washington, DC, police officers used tear gas and other riot-control actions to forcefully remove peaceful protesters from Lafayette Square so that President Trump and senior adminis-tration officials could walk from the White House to St. John's Episcopal Church. When the president's cohort got there, Trump held up a Bible (upside down) and posed for a photo op in front of the church's parish house, which had been damaged by a fire which was set during protests the night before.

Prior to the church visit, Trump had delivered a speech telling U.S. state governors that they needed to stop the BLM protests by using the National Guard to "dominate the streets." If not, he said he would "deploy the United States Military and quickly solve the problem."

The clearing of demonstrators from Lafayette Square was widely condemned as excessive and an attack on the

First Amendment right to peacefully assemble. On May 30, the U.S. Secret Service and U.S. Park Police decided to "establish a more secure perimeter around Lafayette Square and discussed installing an anti-scalable fence." On April 13, 2022, the Department of Justice announced that it reached an agreement to settle claims in four civil cases stemming from the June 1, 2020, BLM protests in Lafayette Square. As a result, guidelines regarding the use of nonlethal force and de-escalation tactics were established. These included requiring officers to wear clearly visible badges and nameplates.

Black Lives Matter Plaza is a two-block-long pedestrian section that was renamed by Washington, DC, Mayor Muriel Bowser on June 5, 2020, after the city's Department of Public Works had painted a thirty-five-foot-tall sign reading, in all caps, "BLACK LIVES MATTER." On June 12, 2020, right-wing religious groups, including the conspiracy-minded Warriors for Christ and the Special Forces of Liberty, filed a federal lawsuit against Mayor Bowser in the United States District Court for the District of Columbia. The suit argued that the Black Lives Matter nonprofit organization was a "cult for secular humanism" and therefore a religious organization. Thus, they contended, Mayor Bowser's renaming of a section of downtown Washington, DC, as Black Lives Matter Plaza violated the separation of church and state. The suit called for the plaza's mural to be removed and its name to be changed to a more secular one, and for the plaza to display different banners, including All Lives Matter, Blue Lives Matter, and Green Lives Matter (for members of the National Guard). The lawsuit was dismissed by Judge Trevor N. McFadden on August 21, 2020, without prejudice. When a similar case was refiled on July 12, 2021, before Judge McFadden, it was also dismissed.

Prior to Trump's 2024 re-election Black Lives Matter Plaza was a popilar public gathering place. Many visitors took photographs of the large yellow letters that represent justice for Black victims of police brutality. After the election, the plaza was sadly removed.

As I write this, Trump's upcoming court schedule looks very full. On February 6, 2024, a federal appeals court in Washington ruled that Trump doesn't have immunity from prosecution in his election case. However, a federal judge delayed Trump's March 4, 2024, trial date on charges he conspired to overturn the 2020 election as the judge awaited a ruling on whether Trump is immune from the charges.

On April 25, 2024, a federal judge upheld the E. Jean Carroll defamation verdict and award of more than $85m against Trump after he called her a liar for accusing him of sexual assault. Carroll, an advice columnist and journalist, originally sued Trump in 2019 for sexually abusing her in a New York City department store in early 1996. In 2023, a jury awarded her with $5mil in compensatory and punitive damages.

Less than a year later, Carroll won a different defamation lawsuit against Trump after he continued to deny her accusations and called her a "political operative." He claimed he had never met her, and said that her memoir, What Do We Need Men For? A Modest Proposal (2019) should be placed in the Fiction section of bookstores. Clearly, he was very upset about what he said were her false claims about the dressing room assault. Thoughts and prayers, Donald. After the verdict was announced, Carroll appeared on several news shows. My favorite thing she said was that Trump was "nothing."

In another case, Trump was accused of falsifying business records connected to a payment made during the final weeks of the 2016 presidential campaign to adult film star Stormy

Daniels. Ms. Daniels had threatened to expose a 2006 sexual encounter with Trump. The case alleges that Daniels was paid $130,000 in hush money by Trump's personal lawyer, Michael Cohen, in October 2016 in exchange for her silence. Trump is also charged in connection with payments made to Playboy model Karen McDougal and a doorman to keep them from sharing stories that could have affected his 2016 presidential election hopes.

On May 30, after a six-week trial and two days of deliberation, a jury in Manhattan, New York, found former President Donald Trump guilty of all 34 felony charges of falsifying business records. Of course, Trump is calling the decision "rigged." His sentencing is scheduled for July 11.

Donald Trump is raising money for his legal fees by selling gaudy Trump sneakers for between $199 and $399 and "God Bless the USA" Bibles (in partnership with country music star Lee Greenwood) for $59.99. In a CNN interview, Georgia senator and ordained minister Raphael Warnock stated, "The Bible does not need Donald Trump's endorsement."

Chapter 9

Christian Nationalism

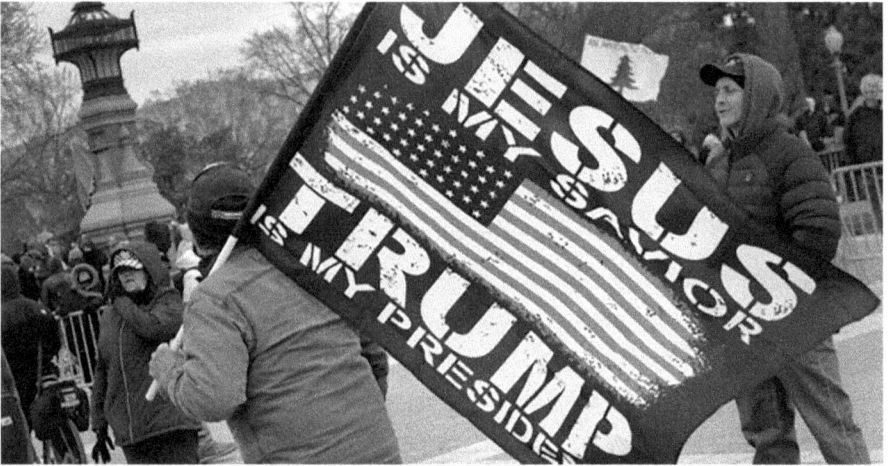

Christian Nationalists at the January 6, 2021 Capitol

The January 6, 2021 events at the U.S. Capitol will forever be etched in my memory. I watched the live stream from my home in northern Virginia (about a half-hour drive away) as a large mob stormed the Capitol. Trump had lost the 2020 election to Joe Biden two months earlier. The goal of these domestic terrorists was to stop a joint session of Congress from counting the electoral votes and thus make Biden's election invalid. The violence that day led to the deaths of five people. Many others were injured, including 174 police officers. Four police officers who responded to the attack died by suicide within the next seven months.

What pissed me off the most while watching this disgusting insurrection were the evangelical "Christians" who carried signs proclaiming messages like "In God We Trust," "Jesus 2020," and "Jesus is my Savior." One of the terrorists carried a Christian flag and another a Bible as they marched through the halls of the Capitol chanting, "The blood of Jesus covering this place."

These evangelicals believed that their only choice was to overthrow the Congress because "evil" forces were taking away their freedom to worship. "We are fighting good versus evil, dark versus light," one evangelical told the New York Times.

The relationship between evangelicals and such a blatantly un-Christian person as Donald Trump is interesting. Some think their devotion stemmed from wanting more conservative Supreme Court justices appointed so the Roe v. Wade decision would be overturned. A lot of them also want school prayer to be reinstated and certain books to be removed from public schools.

In a New Republic article titled "The Capitol Riot Revealed the Darkest Nightmares of White Evangelical America," historian Matthew Avery Sutton wrote:

For the last 150 years, white evangelicals have peddled end-times conspiracies. Most of the time their messages have been relatively innocuous, part of the broader millenarian outlook shared among most major religious traditions. But these conspiracies can have dangerous consequences—and sometimes they lead to violence. Every evangelical generation throughout American history has seen some of its believers driven to extreme conspiracies that blend with other strains of militant political faith. This has meant that in the Trump era, with the destabilizing impact of a global pandemic and a cratered economy, white evangelical Christianity has become enmeshed with, and perhaps inextricable from, a broader revolution against the government.

The insurrection brought attention to the rising White Christian Nationalist movement, closely connected to evangelical Christianity. In seeking to create a White Christian America, Christian Nationalists invoke Christian ideals and words to cover up their hatred of Blacks and non-white immigrants. At the "Save America" rally on the morning of January 6, Paula White, a televangelist, and Trump White House spiritual adviser prayed for God to "give us a holy boldness in his honor." White asked God to "let every adversary against democracy, against freedom, against life, against liberty, against justice, against peace, against righteousness be overturned right now in the name of Jesus."

A few hours later, insurrectionists beat up police officers, battered down barricades and doors, smashed windows, and breached the Senate chamber. In footage captured by The New Yorker, rioters can be seen angrily going through senators' papers and files. They stood on the rostrum of the president of the Senate and thanked God for letting them "send a message to all the tyrants, the communists, and the globalists that this is our nation, not theirs." They proceeded to thank God "for allowing the United States of America to be reborn."

Evangelical leaders decided to blame the violence of that day on Antifa (an anti-fascist group) or Black Lives Matter supporters disguised as MAGA zealots. Of course, this was an outright lie. On the evening after the Insurrection, Michele Bachmann, a former Republican congresswoman, now a dean at the evangelical Regent University, spoke with leaders of the Christian Right in a call to prayer. She told the crowd at the "Save America" rally, "You know the kind of people we were with. The nicest, friendliest, happiest—it was like a family reunion out there. It was incredible, it was wonderful, and then suddenly, this happens." About the rioters at the Capitol, Bachmann insisted that "this wasn't the Trump crowd. This looked nothing like the Trump crowd or the prayer warriors."

A family reunion??!! WTF.

Recently, seventy-one-year-old Rebecca Lavrenz, known on social media as the "J6 Praying Grandma," was convicted on four misdemeanor charges for her activities on January 6. The charges were "entering and remaining in a restricted building or grounds, disorderly conduct in a capitol building, and parading, demonstrating, or picketing in a capitol building."

At the January 6 rally, Lavrenz cited the 1620 Mayflower Compact, which stated that America should be "dedicated to the glory of God" and the "advancement of the Christian faith." Lavrenz said God compelled her to drive across the country: "The whole reason I went to the Capitol was to pray. I didn't get into this for myself. I was there to stand up for my country. God led me to go into the building to stand up for my First Amendment rights and petition the government for a redress of grievances."

Lavrenz faces up to one year in prison and more than$200,000 in fines. She will be sentenced on August 12.

Would real Christians say and do these kinds of things?

Chapter 10

Imagine There're No Hypocrites

Indiana Republican Representative Jim Lucas showing his arsenal to high school student at the Statehouse

As a self-proclaimed hippie, I believe in the power of peace and love. I also believe that all people should be allowed to practice their own choice of religion (or no religion at all). But I will NEVER be ok with the hypocrisy of fake Christians, who insist that they are following the teachings of Jesus, yet support racist, homophobic, and misogynist beliefs and do unholy things that hurt others who don't agree with them. They remind me so much of the things I experienced as a Catholic schoolgirl in the '60s and '70s and the subsequent reports of sexual abuse by so-called representatives of Jesus.

You don't have to look far to find hypocritical Christians in our country today. First, there's Speaker of the House Mike Johnson. He played a big part in trying to overthrow the 2020 presidential results. He's also spoken out against women's and LGBTQ rights. In a 2004 article, Johnson wrote, "Experts project that homosexual marriage is the dark harbinger of chaos and sexual anarchy that could doom even the strongest republic."

Johnson is a proponent of pro-gun policies. Speaking to a Louisiana congregation in 2016, Johnson blamed mass shootings on no-fault divorce laws (he is in a "covenant marriage," which makes divorce more difficult), "radical feminism," and legal abortion. "We've taught a whole generation—a couple of generations, now—of Americans that there is no right and wrong," he said.

On October 5, 2023, Congressman Jamie Raskin of Maryland tweeted the following about Johnson, who would become House Speaker later that month: "Anti-choice, anti-LGBTQ, anti-gun safety, anti-democracy. This is what theocracy looks like." In a New York Times article published just after Johnson's election to the position, Andrew Whitehead, a sociologist at Indiana University-Purdue University Indianapolis, wrote, "Speaker Johnson really does provide a near-perfect example of all the different elements of Christian nationalism," including "being comfortable with authoritarian social control and doing away with democratic values."

In November 2023, Johnson spoke to the National Association of Christian Lawmakers (NACL) gathering at the Museum of the Bible in Washington, DC. He said that during the three weeks of chaos that culminated in his election as Speaker of the House, God woke him up each night and told him he was the new Moses. Johnson also insisted that America is "engaged in a battle between worldviews" that is "a great struggle for the future of the Republic." The specifics of that struggle remained unspoken in Johnson's address. But the NACL's mission, according to materials promoting the gala, includes "abolishing abortion," restoring "traditional marriage between one man and one woman," and "exposing the ungodly effort to undermine our culture by Leftists." Johnson added that he believed far-right Christians would prevail: "We should not be daunted in the face of these challenges. Our hope is in the Lord, our hope, and our trust is in God."

Recently, it was revealed that Johnson wrote the foreword to Scott McKay's racist and homophobic 2022 book, "The Revivalist Manifesto: How Patriots Can Win the Next American Era." The book is full of crazy, unfounded conspiracy theories. Johnson also publicly promoted the book after it was released.

On January 31, 2024, Johnson and other Republican congressional leaders met with Christian leaders, pastors, and evangelists for the second annual National Gathering for Prayer and Repentance. The event occurred on the same day as the bipartisan National Prayer Breakfast in Washington, DC, which has met yearly since 1953. The National Gathering for Prayer and Repentance was advertised as a more right-wing alternative.

According to an article in The Bulwark by Matthew D. Taylor, the National Gathering for Prayer and Remembrance "focused on national penitence and lamenting the many sins of America. It also demonstrated the mainstreaming of the beliefs and values of a new set of insurgent Christian-right leaders—several of whom played major roles in bringing about the violent events of January 6th." During the event, Johnson appeared with pastor Jonathan Cahn, whose sermon implied that abortion and LGBTQ+ health care represent demonic activities.

Another prolific Christian hypocrite is Georgia Republican Representative Marjorie Taylor Greene. Before Greene was elected to Congress, she demonstrated support for political violence, extreme anti-Muslim and anti-Semitic views, and absurd conspiracy theories, including Pizzagate, QAnon, and accusations that Democrats are pedophiles. She also insisted that a plane never hit the Pentagon on September 11, 2001.

At the 2022 Turning Point USA summit in Tampa, Florida Greene identified herself as a Christian Nationalist. Soon, "She is a Nazi" became a popular characterization of Greene on Twitter (now X). Greene responded on Twitter by writing, "I am being attacked by the godless left because I said I'm a proud Christian Nationalist." In a statement sent to "Newsweek" magazine and also shared on Twitter, Greene said, "These evil people are even calling me a Nazi because I proudly love my country and my God. The left has shown us exactly who they are. They hate America, they hate God, and they hate us."

Christian Nationalism espouses the view that America was founded as a Christian nation and, therefore, should be a Christian nation both today and in the future. Christian Nationalists don't believe there should be a separation of church and state in our country. They support putting Christian symbols in public places and making Christmas a stridently Christian national holiday. They advocate teaching the Bible in public schools and posting "In God We Trust" signs in public schools and other public buildings. Overall, Christian Nationalists promote anti-Muslim bigotry, anti-Semitism, and government-sponsored religion. This doesn't sound very Christian to me.

In 2018, before she was elected to Congress, Marjorie Taylor Greene called the Parkland, Florida school shooting, which killed seventeen people and injured seventeen more, a staged event. She accused Parkland survivor and activist David Hogg of being a "paid actor." Hogg cofounded March for Our Lives, the gun control advocacy group. On their website, you can find ways to get involved in the movement, including donating and volunteering. The site also has resources regarding mental health and victims of domestic violence. Other organizations that are working for better gun control laws include Moms Demand Action for Gun Sense in America and the Brady Center to Prevent Gun Violence.

In a video made after Greene joined the House of Representatives, Fred Guttenberg, whose daughter was shot and killed at Parkland's Marjory Stoneman Douglas High School, demanded Greene resign. Social media posts had emerged showing that Greene agreed with people who called the shooting a "false flag" operation. In the posted footage that was recorded before Greene ran for Congress, she is seen following David Hogg as he walks toward the U.S. Capitol to try to change gun laws in our country. She can be heard making false and unfounded claims and asking Hogg a string of ridiculous questions. Hogg wisely continues to walk without answering the questions.

"He's a coward," Greene says at the end of the video as Hogg walks away. She then claims his activism was being funded by billionaire philanthropist George Soros (a popular subject of far-right conspiracy theories) and other liberals. "He can't say one word because he can't defend his stance," she says about Hogg.

Greene—who has also called Hogg "#little Hitler"—said in a written statement to CNN that the video was taken while "I was going from office to office in the Senate to oppose the radical gun control agenda that avid Hogg was pushing." Hogg had a glorious response: "I'm more interested in protecting children and meeting commonsense people who are looking for reasonable solutions to stop children from dying. Don't really have time to help you go viral for attacking survivors so you can fundraise."

Greene is far from the only right-winger who has come close to literally attacking gun control advocates. One of the most disgusting things I've ever seen is a ten-minute video filmed by a student from the Indiana news site the Statehouse File. In the video, filmed in 2020, you can see Indiana state Representative Jim Lucas, a Republican, flashing his gun to a group of students visiting the Indiana Statehouse for Advocacy Day. The students, from the Burris Laboratory School in Muncie, Indiana, were members of Students Demand Action, a national organization made up of young activists calling for action on gun violence. The group was formed after the Parkland shooting. The students were there that day to have discussions with lawmakers about preventing gun violence.

As the students were leaving the Statehouse, Lucas stopped them in the elevator to ask them what they were demanding. When they told him they were pushing for gun sense in America, his response was, "That's terrible." He asked the students to step out of the elevator to have a discussion. Makynna Fivecoats, the student who filmed the video, remembered, "When one of our other members asked why Lucas felt the need to carry a handgun, he showed us his gun, and just at that point, the situation just kind of took a turn. And it was no longer a civil conversation. It was more of a power dynamic. And he was telling us—he was almost talking at us and we just kind of had to sit there and be quiet." Fivecoats said she and the rest of the group members did not feel heard in the situation, adding that adults and lawmakers often overlooked them because of their age.

In the video, Lucas can be heard defending his right to have a handgun, which he said he carries to defend himself. Fivecoats told Lucas that his firearm did not make them feel safe, which led him to say, "OK, those are feelings; I'm talking facts." Fivecoats responded, "That's what this is about. This is about feelings."

In an interview following the incident, Fivecoats said, "The people close to me are dying by guns every day. It is no longer just an adult conversation. It's a me conversation. It's my friend's conversation. It's a school conversation. It's a conversation for everyone, and by him showing me his firearm, it was no longer a conversation but a threat." Lucas had told her, "People who want to kill you don't care about your feelings."

In comments made to the Statehouse File after the incident, Lucas insisted that he was "simply showing an inanimate object" to prove his point about guns. "People that want to have adult conversations, I think, need to be able to handle adult situations," he said. According to the Indianapolis Star, lawmakers are allowed to carry their guns at the Statehouse under state law, and employees are allowed to do so also under a 2017 Senate bill that Lucas helped sponsor.

Unlike Makynna Fivecoats, state Representative Lucas failed to understand that gun violence is a conversation for everyone, including youth. American University recently published a study titled "U.S. Youth Attitudes on Guns". It includes thoughts from more than 4,100 young people across the United States. According to the report, "Young people feel the impact of our country's gun violence crisis firsthand: the average young person in the U.S. knows at least one person who has been injured or killed by a gun. This has a direct effect on their mental health: the more people that youth know who were injured or killed by gun violence, the worse they reported their anxiety, depression, and post-traumatic stress symptoms to be."

Angela Ferrell-Zabala, executive director of Moms Demand Action and senior vice president for movement building at Everytown for Gun Safety, said in the study:

Gun violence is a uniquely American problem—and our young people are bearing the brunt of it. Guns are now the leading cause of death for children, teens and young adults in this country. This report makes it clear that most young people want stronger gun laws, and it's on us to help make that happen. Young people are leading the way in confronting this epidemic and finding solutions, but we can't leave this for the next generation to fix. The findings of this report show the urgent need to address this crisis right now.

In 2023, more than 40,000 people were killed as a result of gun violence. More than half of gun violence deaths that year were deaths by suicide. We need to do much better!

How dare state Representative Lucas behave like he did to these kids? It's clear that he is a mean, sick, and lawless man that shouldn't be allowed to own a gun. Let's look at his storied history.

The Statehouse incident was not the first time Lucas had been at the center of controversy. He has a record of posting controversial comments on his social media accounts. In June 2017, Lucas made offensive comments about rape victims. He claimed that women who carried weapons had learned "how to not be victims." Earlier in 2017, he received criticism for a meme that was seen as making fun of domestic violence victims. In August 2019, Lucas posted a photo of a noose under a photo of a black man convicted of rape. In May of 2020, he posted a meme containing racist stereotypes of black children. In March 2021, Lucas received criticism for comments made about slavery in a Facebook Live video.

In 2021, after Lucas was accused of racist behavior at the Statehouse and on social media, Indiana Speaker of the House Todd Huston removed him from the House Interim Study Committee on Elections and the Interim Study Committee on Public Policy. Lucas was also demoted that year from vice chair to a regular member of the Standing Select Committee on Government Reduction.

Still, Lucas persisted. In a social media post in June 2022, Lucas said that the Robb Elementary School shooting in Uvalde, Texas, was a false flag operation. His comments were compared to those made by the disgraced conspiracy theorist Alex Jones.

Then, on May 31, 2023, the Indiana State Police (ISP) reported that Lucas was arrested after he crashed his vehicle into a guardrail on the I-65 highway near Seymour around midnight. He had left the scene in his vehicle by driving the wrong way down an entrance ramp. He told officers he had swerved to avoid a deer. The ISP reported that officers from the Seymour Police Department found the vehicle parked behind a business located about three miles from the scene of the crash. It had been driven there on two bare rims and a flat tire.

The charges against Lucas were driving while intoxicated and leaving the scene of an accident. Lucas failed multiple field sobriety tests early on May 31. A portable breathalyzer test showed his blood alcohol concentration at .097, higher than the state's legal limit of .08. He also was found to have THC, the active ingredient in marijuana, in his blood. He pleaded guilty to two charges: leaving the scene of an accident, a Class B misdemeanor, and operating a motor vehicle while intoxicated, a Class C misdemeanor. He was handed a 180-day suspended sentence for leaving the scene and a sixty-day suspended sentence on the other charge, and was required to serve one year on probation. As part of his plea agreement, Lucas also was required to complete an alcohol and drug program, pay court and probation fees, and pay nearly $4,000 for crash repairs and restitution to the Indiana Department of Transportation. He also had to attend a victim impact panel, undergo substance abuse screenings, and accept driving restrictions. Speaker Huston said that he wished for Lucas to get "the help that he needs and makes sure that situation doesn't happen again."

On May 7, 2024, Lucas won the Indiana Republican primary to represent District 69. A hypocritical Christian with hypocritical Christian followers...Disgusting!

Last, but certainly not least, is Republican U.S. Representative Lauren Boebert of Colorado, whose outlandishness as a member of Congress rivals Greene's. In a 2022 speech at a Family Camp Meeting conference held at a Colorado Springs church, Boebert joked that Jesus needed an AR-15 to avoid crucifixion. The audience reacted with laughter and cheers.

On December 7, 2021, Boebert had shared a photo on X of her children (all minors) posing in front of their Christmas tree holding large guns. This was only one week after fifteen-year-old Ethan Crumbley had gunned down four classmates and injured several other people at Oxford High School in Michigan.

Crumbley was sentenced to life in prison without parole. His parents were charged with four counts of involuntary manslaughter for their son's actions. Numerous pieces of evidence, including voice mail, social media posts, and text messages, showed that the parents ignored blatant red flags about their son's mental health issues, then bought him a gun and did not safely secure it. Three employees from Jennifer Crumbley's workplace testified against her in court. The witnesses included Jennifer's boss, to whom she said, "He's going to kill himself. He must be the shooter. I need a lawyer. Ethan did it." In another text, Jennifer asked her boss not to judge her for "what my son did."

At a preliminary trial in February 2022, Shawn Hopkins, a counselor at Oxford High School, testified that he met with Ethan to discuss a disturbing homework submission and assess his mental state. During the conversation, Ethan and the counselor discussed Ethan's drawings of a handgun with the words "blood everywhere" written above a person who seemed to be bleeding after being shot twice. A laughing emoji was drawn under the figure. Ethan also wrote, "My life is useless," "The world is dead," and "The thoughts won't stop. Help me."

The counselor later testified that he told the parents that Ethan needed mental health support "as soon as possible, today if possible." In response, Jennifer said she had to return to work that day and that arranging care wouldn't be possible within that time frame. Hopkins stated, "I want him seen within forty-eight hours. I'll be following up." According to the prosecutors, Ethan returned to class after the meeting. At 12:51 p.m. that same day, he came out of a school bathroom with the gun his father had bought four days before and began firing at students in the hallway. On February 6, Jennifer Crumbley was found guilty of four counts of involuntary manslaughter. In March, her husband was also charged and convicted of involuntary manslaughter. They each received a prison sentence of ten to fifteen years.

The Oxford High School tragedy apparently did not shame Lauren Boebert into behaving better. On September 10, 2023, Boebert was famously kicked out of a musical performance of 'Beetlejuice in Denver. According to security footage, she and her male guest were seen vaping, singing, using phones, and causing a disturbance. Boebert denied vaping, although a pregnant woman sitting behind her complained when she saw Boebert doing it. Not a very kind, Christian act.

Boebert's antics are just one symptom of right-wing absurdity. The recent culture wars involving Bud Light beer and the conspiracy theories about singer Taylor Swift are no less insane. In early January 2024, Fox News reporter Jesse Watters asked viewers on his prime-time program if Swift is a "Pentagon asset." After all, she endorsed Biden for president in 2020, and her football star boyfriend Travis Kelce was paid to endorse Pfizer and its COVID-19 vaccine.

"I wonder who's going to win the Super Bowl next month," Vivek Ramaswamy posted on X in late January 2024. "And I wonder if there's a major presidential endorsement coming from an artificially culturally propped-up couple this fall. Just some wild speculation over here, let's see how it ages over the next 8 months." Ramaswamy is a former 2024 presidential candidate known for his conspiracy theories about the January 6 insurrection and the legitimacy of the 2020 election.

"The NFL is totally RIGGED for the Kansas City Chiefs, Taylor Swift, Mr. Pfizer (Travis Kelce)," added Mike Crispi, a Salem Media podcast host. "All to spread DEMOCRAT PROPAGANDA. Calling it now: KC wins, goes to Super Bowl, Swift comes out at the halftime show and 'endorses' Joe Biden with Kelce at midfield."

After an exciting seventy-four minutes and fifty-seven seconds of game play, including overtime, the Kansas City Chiefs were the Super Bowl LVIII champs with a score of 25–22. But the conspiracy theorists were wrong. Taylor Swift didn't come out during the halftime show and endorse Joe Biden. However, she did join Kelce on the field after the game to congratulate him with hugs and kisses. Why would anyone have a problem with that?

Conclusion

"We Can Change the World"
Graham Nash

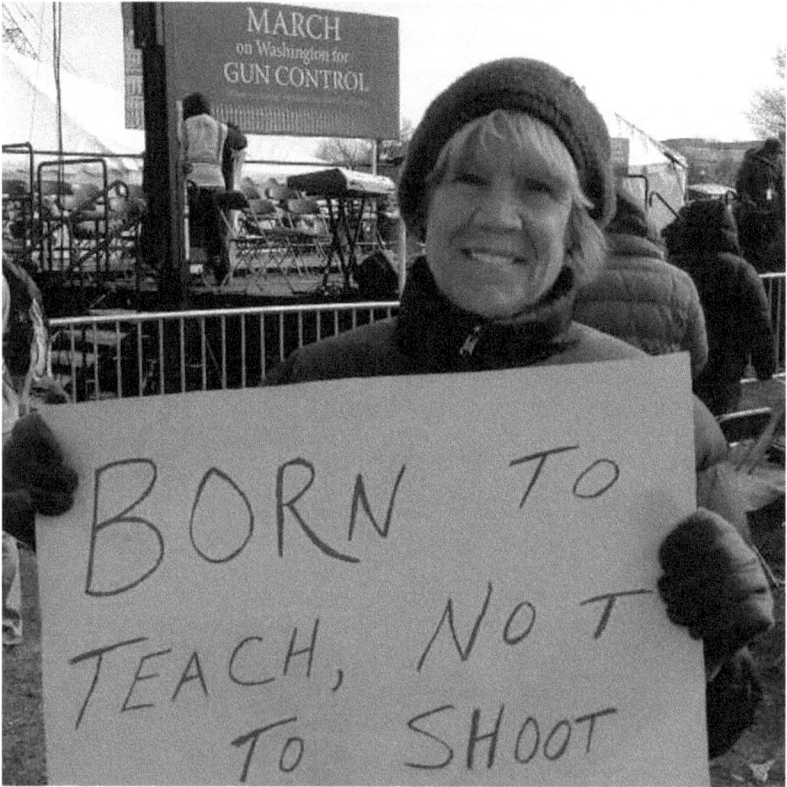

Doing my part to stand up to the hypocrites

A January 2021 survey conducted by the American Enterprise Institute, a conservative think tank, found that more than a quarter of white evangelicals believe that Donald Trump has been secretly battling a "group of child sex traffickers that include prominent Democrats and Hollywood elites." The survey's data also showed that nearly three-quarters of white evangelical Republicans believe widespread voter fraud took place in the 2020 election, compared with 54 percent of non-evangelical Republicans. Other results showed that 60 percent of white evangelical Republicans believe that Antifa, the anti-fascist group, was mostly responsible for the Capitol riot on January 6, compared with 42 percent of non-evangelical Republicans. Other surveys found that white evangelicals are much more skeptical of the COVID-19 vaccine and less likely than other Americans to get it, potentially jeopardizing the country's recovery from the pandemic.

So, what can we do to stop these hypocritical Christians from causing more harm to our country? Doing so may seem impossible, but here are some things that can help:

"Don't boo. Vote!" – Barack Obama

A candidate may be less than perfect but still deserve your vote if he or she supports the rights of all people and doesn't spread conspiracy theories. Please don't stay home on Election Day (unless you can vote by mail). To learn more about registration and voting in your state, go to https://vote.gov/.

Read and watch credible news outlets. As we know, a lot of people get their "news" from various social media brands and shows. It's hard sometimes to discern the truth anymore. On January 1, 2024, the website PureVPN posted an article titled "10 Most Unbiased News Sources in 2024." According to the article, "Honesty," "Fairness," "Accountability," and "Service to Humanity" are the main factors that make a news source trustworthy. Here's their list of unbiased news sources:

Associated Press (AP)

Reuters

NPR

BBC

PBS

Newshour

CBS News

the Guardian

the New York Times

CNN

NBC News

I also recommend Bloomberg and the Washington Post.

Pure VPN's list of biased news sources includes Fox News, Sky News, and Breitbart News. It would be great if all sources of news were required to post their site's bias rating. Purported news outlets that post and broadcast conspiracy theories, lies, and un-Christian hypocrisy should be labeled as "opinion" sources instead of "news." If it ain't the truth, you can't call it news!

The Federal Communications Committee (FCC) has a policy against "news distortion" that it adopted fifty years ago. As discussed in its "The FCC and the First Amendment" guide, the agency is prohibited by law from engaging in censorship or infringing on the First Amendment rights of the press. Those protected rights include, but are not limited to, a broadcaster's selection and presentation of news or commentary.

Unfortunately, the FCC regulation can only be applied to the "broadcast" medium, which usually means over-the-air television or radio networks. This means that the FCC can't enforce it against cable news networks, newspapers or news-letters (whether online or print), social media platforms, online-only streaming outlets, or any other non-broadcast news platform. Another problem is that broadcasters can be subject to sanction only "if they can be proven to have deliberately distorted a factual report." So, if the FCC receives a complaint, they will only investigate if evidence shows that a news outlet's goal is to intentionally mislead its viewers and listeners based on documented written or oral instructions from station management, or evidence of bribery.

So, what can you do if you have a concern or comment about bias in a specific broadcast? The FCC policy is to first contact the station and/or network so that the outlet is aware of the opinions of its audience. If you don't get a response or if you get an inadequate response, you can then file a complaint with the FCC. The fastest way to file a report is directly on the FCC's Consumer Complaint Center home page.

Complaints should include the call sign and community license of the station, the date and time of the broadcast(s) in question, a detailed description of the alleged distorted news, and a transcript or recording.

"Insane in the membrane" – Cyprus Hill

Remember, the crazies are a minority in our country. In an article on Substack titled "Taylor Swift and the Culture Wars," Dan Pfeiffer offers suggestions for combating the deranged culture-wars causes (Bud Light, Taylor Swift, Disney, etc.) that many Christian Nationalists embrace in our country:

First, when taking on an extremist faction, particularly one with authoritarian leanings, it's always helpful to remind the public that this faction is a minority in the country. This helps isolate the threat and rob them of their power. It's also empowering to the rest of us to be reminded that we are the majority. We are not in this fight alone, and we are joined by most of our fellow citizens. Second, having a bizarre meltdown over Taylor Swift, Travis Kelce, and the Super Bowl is fucking weird, and Americans don't elect fucking weirdos. Just ask Ron DeSantis, whose candidacy was doomed the minute people discovered that he eats pudding with his fingers. The Right picking fights with Bud Light is weird. Their opposition to vaccines (which is why they hate Kelce) is weird. Their obsession with trans kids is weird. The fact that the Right focuses on all of the wrong and weirdest things makes them unrelatable to most people.

"Fight the good fight." – John Lewis

Cian O'Mahony, a doctoral student in psychology at University College Cork in Ireland, led a study that was published in the journal PLOS ONE. The authors of the review offer some tips to challenge potentially dangerous conspiracy thinking:

"Don't appeal to emotion. The research suggests that emo-tional strategies don't work to budge belief."

"Don't get sucked into factual arguments. Debates over the facts of a conspiracy theory or the consequences of believing in a particular conspiracy also fail to make much difference."

"Focus on prevention. The best strategies seem to involve helping people recognize unreliable information and untrustworthy sources before they're exposed to a specific belief."

"Support education and analysis. Putting people into an analytic mindset and explicitly teaching them how to evaluate information appears most protective against conspiracy rabbit holes."

The Anti-Defamation League (ADL) features an article on its website titled "Conspiracy Theories and How to Help Family and Friends Who Believe Them." The article explains why these theories are dangerous. They "can sow division, undermine trust in institutions, demonize marginal groups, and be used to justify violence." The article tells what you can do to help family members and/or friends who espouse conspiracy theories. It suggests that you learn more about the origin and claims of the conspiracy theory, ask open-ended questions to encourage critical thinking, and assess the person's health, safety, and well-being. You should offer to find them help, if needed. The ADL's website also has an online bibliography of wonderful children's and young adult books about bias, bullying, diversity, and social justice.

When you see network shows, online posts, and articles that promote racism, misogyny, or homophobia, call them out (as respectfully as possible) by sharing the facts to rebuke them. Join groups and organizations that promote the good things in our country and fight against the bad things. Some of my personal favorites are the Banned Book Club, Everytown for Gun Safety, the National Organization of Women, and the American Civil Liberties Union.

Start or join a Facebook page—or create an account on Twitter (X), Instagram, or a different social media platform—to spread the good news and debunk the fake news. It's a great way to meet like-minded people and to fact-check the conspiracy theorists. Even better, as an administrator, you're able to block the trolls.

Attend rallies, marches, and events to show support for good causes. Being around like-minded activists is good for you! I've attended many events in the Washington, DC, area to advocate for stronger gun control, and women's rights, and immigrants' rights:

At the Patti Smith show at The Anthem DC. September 16, 2023

Education is an essential component of this work. As a teacher and a grandmother, I strongly believe that schools should teach kids the factual history of our country (including topics like slavery). It helps them understand other people and develop empathy. Critical thinking and reading skills should be part of every school's curriculum, starting in kindergarten. In this crazy world of ours, children need to learn how to discern fact from fiction.

Only time will tell whether the children of evangelical Christian parents will stay in the fold or not. I'm thinking (and hoping) that they'll start seeing their parents' hypocrisy, rebel against it, become Taylor Swift (not Kid Rock!) fans, and maybe even go to a drag show. The best and most powerful moments of my life were when I rebelled against my Catholic school hypocrisy and really learned about life.

"They'll know we are Christians by our love." – Father Peter Scholtes

I remember singing this song, written by a Catholic priest, at Mass and in Catholic school in the '60s and '70s. The song's title comes from a line that nonbelievers used to describe the faithful in the early Church: "Behold, how they love one another."

My advice for both believers and nonbelievers is to show kindness, love, and empathy to others, like Jesus did. The organization Random Acts of Kindness has a wealth of information and resources for adults and children alike about the value of performing daily acts of kindness. Research shows that helping others can be good for them, and for our own mental health. It reduces stress, improves our emotional well-being, and even benefits our physical health. It's a win-win

"Don't wanna be an American idiot." – Green Day!

On December 31, 2023, while appearing on Dick Clark's New Year's Rockin' Eve with Ryan Seacrest, the rock group Green Day took aim at Donald Trump. The band tweaked the lyrics to its classic song, "American Idiot." First released in 2004, the song protests the Iraq War-era politics of George W. Bush's presidency. That night, however, lead singer Billie Joe Armstrong changed the original line, "I'm not part of a redneck agenda," to "I'm not part of the MAGA agenda." Of course, the MAGA crowd hated it.

Music has power. At the 2024 Grammy Awards, the unlikely duo of Tracy Chapman and Luke Combs joined together to perform "Fast Car." Over thirty years ago, the song won Chapman the Grammy for Best Pop Vocal Performance. When Combs's version of "Fast Car" earned Song of the Year at the Country Music Awards in 2023, the award went to Chapman as the songwriter, making her the first Black artist to receive the award. In "Fast Car," she shares the feelings of a woman whose life has not turned out the way she had dreamed. The woman quits school and works at a convenience store to pay the bills while her loser boyfriend spends his time hanging out at a bar. She shares her memories and future dream of riding in his fast car to escape. The song became a lesbian anthem when it came out in the late '80s.

The music of the '60s and '70s had a huge effect on the culture and society of the United States. Protest music exposed our country's problems with the help of radio stations that played the songs. There were many social and political issues at the time, including racism, the Vietnam War, police brutality, and feminist activism. One of the largest music festivals of all time was the Woodstock Music and Art Fair, commonly referred to simply as Woodstock. Advertised as "an Aquarian Exposition: 3 Days of Peace & Music," the event was held from August 15 to 18, 1969, on Max Yasgur's dairy farm in Bethel, New York. More than 460,000 people were in attendance at the outdoor show, even though the weather didn't always cooperate. It's now seen as a defining moment for popular music and the counterculture movement, as well as an important event for the silent and baby boomer generations. Unfortunately, my parents believed that, at the age of thirteen, I was too young to attend Woodstock. Bummer!

The importance of the event was highlighted in a 1970 documentary film, also titled "Woodstock", and in the accompanying soundtrack album. Musical events honoring the Woodstock name were held for anniversaries, including the tenth, twenty-fifth, thirtieth, fortieth, and fiftieth anniversary years. In 2004, Rolling Stone magazine ranked the festival as #19 on its list of "50 Moments That Changed the History of Rock and Roll." In 2017, the festival site was listed on the National Registry of Historic Places.

We need a 2024 music festival! Artists like Green Day, Taylor Swift, Kendrick Lamar, Jay-Z, Common, John Legend, Tom Morello, Patti Smith, Dolly Parton, Billie Eilish, Beyoncé, and others who share our concerns and offer solutions can give us hope for the future. I'm pretty sure it would be a sellout, and I'm also pretty sure that evangelical Christians would hate it. But maybe their kids would find a way to attend.

I'll keep my fingers crossed and hope for the best. As I said earlier, I'm an eternal optimist.

PS: Here's a link to my Spotify playlist, in case you were curious! (Please note that I don't own the rights to these songs).

Note to Readers:

The most difficult part of writing this book for me was finishing it. Every day, crazy, hypocritical people are doing crazy, hypocritical things.

The recent antics involving Supreme Court justices have caused many Americans to lose trust in the "highest court in the land." When their neighbors in Alexandria, Virginia complained about the upside-down flag hanging from his house on January 17, 2021, Alito quickly blamed his wife, Martha Ann. The flag brought back the traumatic scenes of that terrible day at the Capitol on January 6, 2021, when some protestors carried inverted flags to show support for Trump and his false claim that the election was "stolen" from him illegally.

In taped interviews by Lauren Windsor of Politico Magazine, Martha Ann is heard saying that she fantasized about designing a flag featuring the Italian word, 'vergogna," meaning shame, to make a statement against people flying LGBTQ pride flags across the lagoon from their New Jersey vacation home during Pride Month.

Then there's Project 2025, the Presidential Transition Project,produced by the conservative group, Heritage Foundation. This project has four main goals:

1.To restore the family as the centerpiece of American life

2.To dismantle the administrative state

3.To defend the nation's sovereignty and borders

4.To secure God-given individual rights to live freely.

This 900-page detailed authoritarian playbook maps out extremist policies on such topics as health care, abortion rights, and overtime pay and education.

A recent Louisiana law requiring public schools to display the Ten Commandments in every classroom in schools and colleges in the state is insane! Have they not heard about the separation of church and state? Do they know that there are children who are not being raised as "Christians?" I've taught students from many different religious backgrounds, and some from no religious backgrounds. This is so disrespectful to them.

The violent rhetoric and evil threats fueled by Trump are beyond frightening. The attacks against politicians and people like Manhattan District Attorney Alvin Bragg, Fulton County District Attorney Fani Willis, the Georgia election workers, and many others who are decent Americans just doing their jobs are truly scary. "Swatting" incidents have sadly become everyday events in our country. Swatting, a federal crime, usually punished by a felony, is when someone calls emergency services with a fake accusation about a person committing a crime at the victim's house. This leads to a response from law enforcement with the very real possibility of dangerous outcomes.

This week, President Biden and Donald Trump will meet in the first of two debates. This one will be televised on CNN. There's a lot of speculation about how effective these two "older" men will be on the debate stage, and people are making predictions (and probably bets) about who will be the winner. If anything, the debates will be interesting. Time to buy popcorn!

Afterword

Shortly after this book was published, Trump won the 2024 presidential election. Two days later, one of my Facebook groups was hacked and taken over. I had over 260,000 like-minded followers on the page I started in 2016 when Hillary ran for election. So now, I'm not only horrified about another Trump presidency, but I'm also extremely pissed off.

After I screamed and cried for a few days, I'm more energized than ever. As Marilyn Monroe once said, "Strong women don't have attitudes, we have standards."

It's obvious that I'll have a lot to bitch and moan about during the next four years, probably enough to write at least a few more books. In the words of one of my favorite punk rockers from the 1970s, Patti Smith, "People Have the Power."

Stay tuned…

List of Sources by Chapter

Chapter 3

The Guardian. "Author Khaled Hosseini on Book Bans in the US: 'It Betrays Students.'" February 13, 2024. https://www.theguardian.com/books/2024/feb/13/khaled-hosseini-us-book-bans- interview#:~:text=%E2%80%9CBanning%20books%20doesn't%20 protect,in%20Europe%20in%20 the%201930s.

PEN America. "New Report Finds Unprecedented Surge in School Books Bans." April 16, 2024. https://pen.org/press-release/new-report-find-unprecedented-surge-in-school-books- bans/#:~:text=PEN%20America%20has%20 documented%20over,%2C%20sexual%20violence%2C%20 and%20rapechic.

Urban Dictionary. "Woke." https://www.urbandictionary.com/define.php?term=Woke. Yurcaba, Jo. "Missouri Republican Candidate Torches LGBTQ-inclusive Books in Viral Video." NBC News. Feb. 7, 2024. https://www.nbcnews.com/nbc-out/out-politics-and-policy/missouri-republican-candidate-torches-lgbtq-inclusive-books-viral-vide-rcna137715.

Chapter 4

Bunch, Will. "How Trump Became All of America's Frank Rizzo." Philadelphia Inquirer. November. 17, 2020. https://www.inquirer.com/columnists/attytood/trump-frank-rizzo-transition-of-power-election-20201117.html.

Henley, Jon. "How the Boston Globe Exposed the Abuse Scandal that Rocked the Catholic Church." Boston Globe. April 21, 2010. https://www.theguardian.com/world/2010/apr/21/boston-globe-abuse-scandal-catholic.

Lee, Michelle Ye Hee. "'Rapists?' Criminals? Checking Trump's Facts." Philadelphia Inquirer. July 9, 2015. https://www.inquirer.com/philly/news/politics/20150709__Rapists__ _Criminals__Checking_Trump_s_facts.html.

National Review Board for the Protection of Children and Young People. A Report on the Crisis in the Catholic Church in the United States. Feb. 27, 2004. https://www.usccb.org/issues-and-action/child-and-youth-protection/upload/a-report-on-the-crisis-in-the-catholic-church-in-the-united-states-by-the-national-review-board.pdf.

NBC News. "Donald Trump Makes Lewd Remarks about Women on Video." October. 7, 2016. https://youtu.be/fYqKx1GuZGg?si=SRhonn2wWjcNNutz. NBC News. "Donald Trump on 2005 Tape: 'This Was Locker Room Talk.'" Oct. 9, 2016. https://www.youtube.com/watch?v=IEOO0MjhVsU.

Philadelphia Inquirer. "The Moments That Made Frank Rizzo Philly-famous." August 21, 2017. https://www.inquirer.com/philly/news/pennsylvania/philadelphia/phill y-history/frank-rizzo-top-moments-philadelphia-history.html.

Severns, Maggie. "Trump: 'I Was Going to Say Something Extremely Rough' to Clinton." Politico. September. 26, 2016. https://www.politico.com/story/2016/09/what-was-trump-going-to-say-to-clinton-first-debate-228744.

Taubman, Philip. "U.S. Files Its Rights Suit Charging Philadelphia Police with Brutality." New York Times. Aug. 14, 1979 https://www.nytimes.com/1979/08/14/archives/us-files-its-rights-suit-charging-philadelphia-police-with.html.

Trump, Donald J. Twitter (X) post. Oct. 11, 2016. https://x.com/realDonaldTrump/status/785842546878578688.

Yan, Holly. "Donald Trump's 'Blood' Comment about Megyn Kelly Draws Outrage." CNN. Aug. 8, 2015. https://www.cnn.com/2015/08/08/politics/donald-trump-cnn-megyn-kelly-comment/index.html.

Chapter 8

Alberta, Tim. The Kingdom, the Power, and the Glory: American Evangelicals in an Age of Extremism. New York: HarperCollins, 2023.

Cohen, Michael. Disloyal: A Memoir: The True Story of the Former Personal Attorney to President Donald J. Trump. New York: Skyhorse, 2020.

Office of Inspector General U.S. Department of the Interior. Review of U.S. Park Police Actions at Lafayette Park. June 8, 2021. https://www.doioig.gov/reports/review/review-us-park-police-actions-lafayette-park.

Oprihory, Jennifer-Leigh. "President to Governors: Deploy Guard, 'Dominate the Streets.'" Air & Space Forces. June 1, 2020. https://www.airandspaceforces.com/over-17000-guard-personnel-responding-to-civil-unrest-across-the-u-s/.

The Real Woodstock Story. "An Aquarian Exposition at Woodstock 1969." http://www.woodstockstory.com/aquarianexposition.html.

Rolling Stone. "50 Moments That Changed Rock and Roll: Otis and Jimi Burn It Up." June 24, 2004. https://www.rollingstone.com/music/music-news/50-moments-that-changed-rock-and-roll-otis-and-jimi-burn-it-up-179338/.

Villarreal, Daniel. "Group Sues D.C. Mayor Over Street Mural, Says It Violates Freedom of Religion Clause on Behalf of 'Black Lives Matter Cult.'" Newsweek. June 15, 2020. https://www.newsweek.com/group-sues-dc-mayor-over-street-mural-says-it-violates-freedom-religion-clause-behalf-1510617#:~:text=The%20group%20Warriors%20for%20Christ,%2 2Black%20Lives%20Matter%20cult.%22.

Chapter 9

Sutton, Matthew Avery. "The Capitol Riot Revealed the Darkest Nightmares of White Evangelical America." The New Republic. January 14, 2021. https://newrepublic.com/article/160922/capitol-riot-revealed-darkest-nightmares-white-evangelical-america.

U.S. House of Representatives Select Committee to Investigate the January 6th Attack on the United States Capitol. "Christian Nationalism and the Capitol Insurrection: Written Testimony of Andrew L. Seidel of the Freedom from Religion Foundation on the Role Christian Nationalism Played in the Lead Up to and during the Attack of January 6th." March 18, 2022. https://www.govinfo.gov/content/pkg/GPO-J6-DOC-CTRL0000062431/pdf/GPO-J6-DOC-CTRL0000062431.pdf.

Chapter 10

CBS (AP). "Taylor Swift, Travis Kelce Conspiracy Theories Abound on Political Right with K.C. Chiefs in Super Bowl." Feb. 2, 2024. https://www.cbsnews.com/news/taylor-swift-travis-kelce-conspiracy-theories-chiefs-super-bowl/.

Chamlee, Virginia. "Chorus of Condemnation Grows for New Congresswoman Seen

Badgering Parkland Shooting Survivor." Yahoo! News (People). Jan. 29, 2021. https://uk.news.yahoo.com/chorus-condemnation-grows-congresswoman-seen-191606261.html?

guce_referrer=aHR0cHM6Ly93d3cuZ29vZ2xlLmNvbS8&guce_re
_sig=AQAAAFeeaDi8e23ZvBupKmgavM0wAYUaTbqzwzWOKvp3
9YDXU_sJAxuRIAyn8Fr8mx4pmilRrdpEIvadddXS3LamSt4TZ9c4
J5EeQPPPwj3khYGEYJbdLA816tPgeZv0egHNzZEaf1oM1deby5Z
sBnIP13mTDz1p.

C-SPAN. "Representative Taylor Greene at Turning Point USA Conservative Conference." December. 19, 2021. https://www.c-span.org/video/?516849-5/representative-taylor-greene-turning-point-usa-conservative-conference.

Dicker, Ron. "Jesse Watters Floats Goofy Right-Wing Theory about Taylor Swift: 'That's Real.'" Yahoo! News (Huffpost). Jan. 10, 2024. https://sg.news.yahoo.com/jesse-watters-floats-goofy-wing-161648717.html.

Dickinson, Tim. "Mike Johnson Compares Himself to Moses at Christian Nationalist Gala." Rolling Stone. Dec. 6, 2023. https://www.rollingstone.com/politics/politics-news/mike-johnson-moses-christian-nationalist-gala-1234918565/.

Fung, Katherine. "Pastor Warns about Marjorie Taylor Greene: She 'Dances with the Devil.'" Newsweek. July 30, 2022. https://www.newsweek.com/marjorie-taylor-greene-christian-nationalism-reverend-chuck-currie-1728815.

Garrity, Kelly. "'The Bible Does Not Need Donald Trump's Endorsement.'" Politico. March 31, 2024. https://www.politico.com/news/2024/03/31/warnock-trump-bible-2024-elections-00149855.

Goldiner, Dave. "Vivek Ramaswamy Says Super Bowl Could Be Rigged to Boost Taylor Swift—and Biden." New York Daily News. Jan. 29, 2024. https://www.nydailynews.com/2024/01/29/vivek-ramaswamy-says-super-bowl-could-be-rigged-to-boost-taylor-swift-and-biden/#:~:text=%E2%80%9CI%20wonder%20who's%20going%20to,%2Dup%20couple%20this%20fall.%E2%80%9D

Hosseini, Fatema and Parker Leipzig. "Most Maryland House Democrats See New House Speaker as Extremist, Threat to Democracy." Capital News Service. Oct. 26, 2023. https://cnsmaryland.org/2023/10/26/most-maryland-house-democrats-see-new-house-speaker-as-extremist-threat-to-democracy/.

Howard, Kyra. "Lucas Responds to Gun-flash Controversy by Offering Safety Course to Teens." TheStatehouseFile.com. Feb. 13, 2024. https://www.thestatehousefile.com/politics/lucas-responds-to-gun-flash-controversy-by-offering-safety-course-to-teens/article_5ed39ae4-cab1-11ee-a810-ff8581ff00c7.html.

Kaczynski, Andrew and Allison Gordon. "New Speaker of the House Mike Johnson Once Wrote in Support of the Criminalization of Gay Sex." CNN. Oct. 27, 2023. https://www.cnn.com/2023/10/25/politics/mike-johnson-gay-sex-criminalization-kfile/index.html.

Kaczynski, Andrew and Em Steck. "Speaker Johnson Wrote Foreword for Book Filled with Conspiracy Theories and Homophobic Insults." CNN. Dec. 1, 2023. https://www.cnn.com/2023/12/01/politics/kfile-mike-johnson-conspiracy-theories-homophobic-slurs/index.html.

Karni, Annie, Ruth Graham, and Steve Eder. "For Mike Johnson, Religion Is at the Forefront of Politics and Policy." New York Times. Oct. 27, 2023. https://www.nytimes.com/2023/10/27/us/politics/mike-johnson- speaker-religion.html.

Ly, Laura, Holly Yan, and Amir Vera. "Judge Rules That Ethan Crumbley's Parents Will Stand Trial for Involuntary Manslaughter." CNN. Feb. 24, 2022. https://www.cnn.com/2022/02/24/us/ethan-crumbley-parents-michigan-shooting/index.html.

Morales, Mark, Laura Ly, and Eric Levenson. "Mom of Michigan School Shooting Suspect Pleaded to Keep Job Shortly after the Shooting, Boss Says." WBAL-TV (CNN). Feb. 9, 2022. https://www.wbaltv.com/article/jennifer-crumbley-mom-michigan-school-shooting-suspect-boss-text-messages/39027441.

Ramirez, Nikki McCann. "New House Speaker Blamed School Shootings on Teaching Evolution and Abortion." Rolling Stone. Oct. 26, 2023. https://www.rollingstone.com/politics/politics-news/mike-johnson-blamed-shootings-teaching-evolution-abortion-1234863223/.

Smith, Brandon. "House Speaker Huston Says Lucas Shouldn't Have Flashed Holstered Gun at Students." WFYI. Feb. 1, 2024. https://www.wfyi.org/news/articles/house-speaker-huston-says-lucas-shouldnt-have-flashed-holstered-gun-at-students.

Taylor, Matthew D. "Mike Johnson Is Mainstreaming the Spirituality that Gave Us the Capitol Riot." The Bulwark. Feb. 06, 2024. https://www.thebulwark.com/p/mike-johnson-mainstreaming-jan-6th-spirituality?utm_source=publication-search.

Tuft, Jim. "Rep. Jim Lucas Shows His Gun to Kids at Statehouse. Yes, He's Allowed to Carry One There." Indianapolis Star. Feb. 1, 2024. https://www.indystar.com/story/news/2024/01/31/indiana-rep-jim-lucas-republican-gun-laws-statehouse-general-assembly-2024-seymour/72422259007/.

Conclusion

Anti-Defamation League. "Conspiracy Theories and How to Help Family and Friends Who Believe Them." Aug. 23, 2022. https://www.adl.org/conspiracy-theories? gad_ Pappas, Stephanie. "Conspiracy Theories Can Be Undermined with These Strategies, New Analysis Shows." Scientific American. April 5, 2023. https://www.scientificamerican.com/article/how-can-you-fight-conspiracy-theories/. _____ Pfeiffer, Dan. "Taylor Swift and How to Win the Culture War." The Message Box. Feb. 01, 2024. https://www.messageboxnews.com/p/taylor-swift-and-how-to-win-the-culture.

PureVPN. "10 Most Unbiased News Sources in 2024." April 1, 2024. https://www.purevpn.com/blog/unbiased-news-sources/.

The Real Woodstock Story. "An Aquarian Exposition at Woodstock 1969."

Rolling Stone. "Remembering Woodstock: Why the 1969 Festival Still Resonates." Aug. 1, 2019. https://www.rollingstone.com/music/music-news/woodstock-remembered-video-country-joe-david-fricke-greil-marcus-866139/.

Zhan, Jennifer. "Green Day Shaded Trump (Again) on New Year's Eve." Vulture. Jan. 1, 2024. https://www.vulture.com/2024/01/green-day-shades-trump-maga-agenda-new-years-eve-performance.html.

www.ingramcontent.com/pod-product-compliance
Lightning Source LLC
Chambersburg PA
CBHW052118030426
42335CB00025B/3041